PENGUIN BOOKS

THE WORLDS WITHIN YOU

Shreya Ramachandran grew up in Chennai and studied South Asian literature and history. She writes about mental health on her blog, and her work has also appeared in *The Hindu*, the *Swaddle* and *Spark* magazine. She currently lives in Mumbai with an indie dog who behaves part cat. This is her first novel.

ADVANCE PRAISE FOR THE BOOK

'Sensitive, observant, and honest, *The Worlds Within You* is a touching debut from a young writer to watch'—Anjali Joseph, author of *Saraswati Park*

'Moving and elegiac, a first novel with a fine old heart'—Siddharth Dhanvant Shanghvi, author of *Loss*

'A wonderfully written, clear-eyed novel about growing up, learning to live with yourself, your family and your memories. Moving, funny and incredibly real'—Shabnam Minwalla, author of *When Jiya Met Urmila*

'Tender and deceptively simple, *The Worlds Within You* is microscopically observed and at the same time has that quality of universality that sets apart good literature from merely passable literature. This may not be a 'unique' novel in terms of plot or ideas, but a good writer—a title Shreya Ramachandran has earned with this book—can make even the most quotidian subject matter interesting and affecting'—Roshan Ali, author of *Ib's Endless Search for Satisfaction*

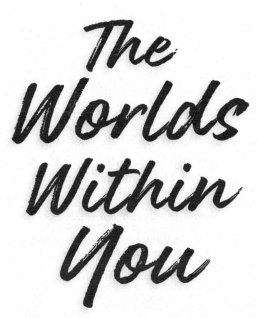

The Worlds Within You

SHREYA RAMACHANDRAN

PENGUIN BOOKS

An imprint of Penguin Random House

PENGUIN BOOKS

USA | Canada | UK | Ireland | Australia
New Zealand | India | South Africa | China

Penguin Books is part of the Penguin Random House group of companies
whose addresses can be found at global.penguinrandomhouse.com

Published by Penguin Random House India Pvt. Ltd
4th Floor, Capital Tower 1, MG Road,
Gurugram 122 002, Haryana, India

First published in Penguin Books by Penguin Random House India 2022

Text copyright © Shreya Ramachandran 2022
Illustration copyright © Nandita Ratan 2022

All rights reserved

10 9 8 7 6 5 4 3 2 1

ISBN 9780143453338

Typeset in Cormorant Garamond by Manipal Technologies Limited, Manipal

www.penguin.co.in

At the moment I am finding it a little difficult, because it is all too new. I am a beginner in the circumstances of my own life

Rainer Maria Rilke

Prologue

Chennai, September 2006.

Shouldn't it be breezy and rainy? It was warm, like the weather was on pause. Downstairs, everyone gathered for my grandfather Thatha's funeral. They were talking about the show timings at the Mayajaal movie theatre; whether anyone remembered to call Roja, was she coming herself or did someone have to pick her up; did someone call the caterer for the tenth-day meal.

Appa knocked at my door. I was lying on the bed, staring out at the trees. Appa appeared near my bed, wearing linen shorts and sandals. He looked like he was going to the beach, not to Thatha's cremation.

'Come,' Appa said. He scrabbled over my blanket to find my hand and held it.

'I don't want to, Appa. I hate seeing everyone's faces.'

Sam slunk out from behind Appa and came and sat on my bed. 'I agree,' Sam said to Appa. She got in next to me and hugged me while lying entirely on top of me like a whale.

Her gangly limbs stretched all across me. Her chin left little sharp indents in my shoulder.

'Sam is arranging photo frames in the hall. Amma printed out a nice photo with the background blurred out and Thatha's looking handsome in it. Come see.'

'No, Pa.'

'Sam, go downstairs quickly,' Appa said. 'I'll come downstairs in one minute.'

Appa's hand was warm on mine. He got up to leave. 'I want you to write a poem about Thatha, okay? Can be anything you want,' Appa said. 'You're always scribbling in your notebook, no?'

My notebook was a 2005 planner with the date and day in navy blue on every page, with a helpful 'Thought for the Day' under it. Today's thought: *He not busy being born is busy dying—Bob Dylan.* It was Thatha's, and the first few pages had his writing, in Tamil I only half-understood.

Sakala Kalavali Maalai.

As he neared the door, Appa used the bottom of his shirt to clean my switchboard, wiping the top free of dust. 'You think Thatha would want you to just sit in your room like this?'

'I don't know. How would I know?' Would I ever know?

Appa shut the door behind him, pausing before it closed.

Prologue

In the evening, once everyone had left, Amma, Appa and Sam came into my room.

Amma took the diary from me and read out:

'Everyone waits for it to rain.
Like the sun and the clouds are crying.
But it stays hot, the air like thick blankets made of wool.
Something's changed. Is it something here?
Something you left before you went?
I sometimes wish . . .'

'That's all?' Appa asked.

'It's fine, Ami, take some rest. Let's go, Shekar; give her some space, no?' Amma said.

Sam and Amma slipped out of the room.

'Finish it, baby,' Appa said as he left.

*

1

A gap term, my father points out, is meant to be just a 'term'.

We are sitting around the table at home in Adyar, Chennai. It's November 2013. Sam and Appa are eating idlis, their elbows all spread out amidst newspapers. Amma flits from the dining table to the kitchen. Appa is discussing my gap term and absence from college. It started as a week and is now over a month, threatening to spill into the new year because I 'don't know' whether I'll go back in January.

Appa does not want such ambiguities. I look to Amma for help, but she's too busy talking to someone on her headphones. I hear a rumble, rather than individual words, of what she is saying.

I sometimes truly wish I could be Amma. I was born with basically no idea of what to say at any time. I spend all my time worrying about things that won't even happen. Is there a 'Norms of Comportment'-type book that exists somewhere, and does everyone have it except me?

'So, totally how many classes you've missed?' Appa asks. He says this all enjambed, all one sentence.

'One month's worth,' Sam speaks instead of me. As usual, I have an unfortunate habit of not speaking when I need to.

'And they said you can go back in January, no? Ami? What did the dean say?'

I think about what I will write in my journal later this evening about this conversation, in my room, which used to be Thatha's room. Thatha had moved into the ground floor guest room, I moved into his old room upstairs, and Sam finally got her own room, which she said she needed so that she could 'unwind'.

'The dean told her she can just start in Jan and miss a term and graduate one term late, Appa,' Sam says, solemnly smearing nei all over her plate and then laying her idli flat in it.

'When did she say that?' Appa asks.

'I don't remember,' I say.

'You don't—'

'Recently only, Pa. I think a week ago,' Sam says.

'Then write, tell her, "Melanie—"'

'Marjorie,' I correct.

'Same thing. Say, "Can I please confirm that I will start in Jan, is there any form I have to fill or any other formalities to be done", and say, "hope you are well, kind regards",' Appa says.

'I don't say "kind regards",' I say.

'I asked in school,' Sam says, 'and they said Ami can teach. I asked Sharon Ma'am and everything.'

'Practice for my own story,' I say.

'What story?' Appa asks.

'I'm writing about Thatha.'

'What about him?' Appa continues. 'Anyway, that writing class is one day a week. It can't be the only thing you do.'

'She's getting paid, Pa,' Sam says. I've lost my voice and am instead looking at the edge of my plate, where the oil meets the steel, the little reflections of golden. Ideally, I would be able to say things. I do have thoughts. But they just dissolve like sugar at the edge of my throat.

'What pay, some 5000 rupees they'll pay,' Appa says. Amma is laughing in the kitchen at a joke I wish I knew. Sam and I look at each other. This is not great.

'What,' Appa says. 'How much are they paying?'

'Um,' I say. 'It's not . . .' It is fairly close to his estimate.

'Come here, come here,' he says.

Sam and I tiptoe around the table, filled with plates, newspapers, charging cables, half-crumpled pieces of paper and Appa's laptop. We crowd around him like he is a bonfire on a cold, non-Chennai night while Amma comes back, takes my plate before I'm done eating, and gets up to put the dishes in the sink. Spoons, half-drunk water glasses and oil bowls clatter.

'Hema, come,' Appa says.

Outside, cycle bells and revving cars provide background music. One car reverses to the tune of A.R. Rahman's Airtel song, the last creature in the world to still use that song.

'Who do you think made the spreadsheet?' Amma asks. 'Why should I see it again?' Amma's voice echoes—she is everywhere, her voice reaching the rafters. She's in the kitchen again.

He shows us a set of grids and numbers. 'Salary,' he says. 'Total income. Then projected expenses for the next few years. Total savings minus what we usually spend. Your mother and I only have money for the next ten years. That's it. See?'

I nod. I look at the box that shows when his money runs out. I can't even imagine reaching that point. Five years, ten years, twenty years later.

'What's that little number?' Sam asks, her finger leaving a smudge on the laptop screen.

'Move your hand, Sammy,' Appa says, scrubbing the smudge with the cuff of his shirt. 'That's the expected inflation rate. So more of our money will go.'

'Ohh,' Sam says.

'Got it?' Appa asks me, closing the laptop. Sam and I return to our seats.

I look over at Appa. He has grey hair at his temples. They arrived when he turned fifty, like a birthday present. The sun glints against his head. *Stay calm*, I tell myself. *Not bad, you have the presence of mind to say 'stay calm' at least, even if you can't.*

'You know what Ami's dean said?' Appa asks Amma, when she swans into the room. Amma puts her finger on her lips. She is still on the phone, headphones glinting red in her ears.

I can picture Thatha sitting there, on the sofa, reading the newspaper, folding the page down to a square as he reads it, then reopening it to its full size and turning the page, the top caving and folding in.

Thatha loved his evening walks. All set with his aviator sunglasses, his white *veshti*, his stick to keep stray dogs away, his thick leather chappals. One day, Amma got a call from someone who saw him fall by the side of the road. She drove back home and took Thatha to

5

the hospital. Then she came home and gave us dinner, which Appa had cooked.

'We have to move him,' Amma had said. She crumpled the newspapers into large cones, when she swept them off the table to make space for food. 'To the orthopaedic hospital. They're experts.' She poured us all water, the sound startling, the glasses shaking. The tablecloth was dotted with dried, cracked turmeric stains, like parched earth. I plucked at them. I was nauseous, tired, hungry, unable to eat. Sam ate by the spoonful.

'Can I come meet him, Amma?' Sam asked, in between bites.

'Not yet, baby. Let him have the surgery, then recover.'

'What's wrong with surgery at this hospital?' Appa asked. He looked across the dining room, as if he could see through the wall, into Thatha's room.

'Your uncle only said the specialist hospital is better,' Amma said. 'Did *I* say it?'

'Why you are snapping at me is what I fail to understand,' Appa said.

'You can't take your time with this decision, Shekar.'

Present day. Sam eating. She wipes her hands on her shorts, but they are still sticky. With her fingers covered with the squishy melted parts of idli, she scrapes all the chutney to the edge of her plate, and then scoops it up and licks her hand.

Amma looms over me and sees on my phone a photograph I took from the plane: squares of edited deep blue, and dots of pastel houses across the bottom of the frame: banana yellow, pastel pink, pista green, lavender purple, all interspersed with swaying palm and coconut and casuarina trees.

I play with the photo, moving in closer so the trees and the flat tops of the terraces, concrete-washed, are right before my eyes.

'Old Mahabalipuram,' Amma says to me, about the photo.

'Oh, really?'

'We can go. I can take you,' Amma says.

'I'm sure it only looks nice from the sky, Ma,' I say.

7

'So what do you want me to do?' Amma asks.

'I didn't say you had to do anything . . .'

Sam is swiftly moving, on lithe feet, to her room door.

'I finished eating, okay, Ma?' Sam says. 'I'm going to go put my ironed clothes into my cupboard.'

She goes into the kitchen with her plate, washes it and keeps it on the drying rack. Then, with footsteps that make no sounds, she slowly slips upstairs. She is gone, saving herself from any fights, to unwind.

*

2

'Ready?' Sam asks.

'Sam.' I am at the edge. I am at the very edge of the steps and below, the beautiful sight of the dirty Adyar River stretches like a ribbon. 'I think I forgot how to do this.'

'Don't be scared. Jump.'

We jump down the last three stairs, on to the coarse green grass below. Wet mud collects at our toes.

I don't know why we loved playing this game when we were small: taking the shortcut from our balcony to the ledge outside, above the garden. Trying to jump from the ledge on to the garden, and landing on our feet.

Like cats.

'Now, time to cycle,' Sam says.

'My cycle doesn't have air.'

'It does. I filled it.'

'But I'm tired and I'm not wearing the right shoes and . . .'

Sam starts walking, her chappals flapping, around the garden to the side of the building. Against the fading paint of the electrical shed, cycles lean, tired, dusty. We pick ours up.

I remember when this was enough: me and Sam and a purple, mosquito-filled evening. I used to cycle and feel so free, so powerful, so happy. I was small, the world and the roads were wide and sweeping, a whirlwind around me, and if I dreamt something, it was enough to make it real.

'Shit,' I say. 'The seat is so hard. It hurts.'

'Ami,' Sam says.

Up the side of the shed, little red ants climb straight up. From afar, they're a crack in the cement, or maybe a fallen tree fibre or a trick of the light. But from up close, each ant is moving. They're big red ants, not the small red ones that bite. Next to them are the even more harmless, big black ants.

Sam and I used to bend down and look at every big ant, see if it would climb on to our palm, poke at it with a stick, see how far on its track we could follow it. We'd crouch, like archaeologists or ducks. Minutes would pass—no ticking of the clock—no movement. Just time suspended.

When did that stop?

When did that go away?

I feel warm tears at the edge of my eyes, and when Sam looks at me, I say, 'Look, ants.'

'Ey, look. The big ones,' Sam says. She is already lifting her leg on to her cycle. 'Come.'

Sam is swerving, and I'm lingering behind. Then, when the wind is blowing right, I cycle past the evening walkers, the city government workers, the security guards, the idling cars. The road is a carpet, dotted with copper pod flowers and twigs. It drizzled in the afternoon, so the roads are wet, a dark grey, and there are fallen branches of trees piled up like firewood on the sides of the road. The weather is neither hot nor cold. The air smells like the river, like sweet garbage. We cycle around the road, take the side alley and come back down: we go in big swooping circles.

When we are on a quiet patch of road—past the embassy and before the right turn—I find the exact pace of pedalling where the pedals basically move themselves, and I release my hands from the handlebars.

The cycle sways a little, turning to the left, to the right— then it settles. I'm cycling, straight line, hands free.

When I first taught myself this trick, Sam made me do it again and again. Thatha would be walking on the side of the road, crisp white shirt, half-laughing, looking up, talking to another evening walker. His hands would be raised up, and he would shake them: *Don't do it, ma. What if you fall?*

His sunglasses shone in his shirt pocket and his eyes crinkled when he smiled and he would wave before us as we swerved, and I would teach Sam how to do it: *see, just balance your hand above the handlebar, now let go, now you'll tilt but you won't fall.* She almost fell once or twice, but she stopped herself. Her foot hit the ground before the pedal did. Then she got up. On some days, she used to sit on the back seat of my cycle, if she was tired or if I was feeling grand, a boatman ferrying people to the farthest shore.

'Can you do it if I'm sitting on your cycle? Or will it be too heavy? Can you try?' And I would try. But I'd lurch forward and then put my hands back on the handlebars, just in time, the rubber ridging against my palms, catching the pedals again as they were wheeling of their own will.

Sam knows the trick too, now. She swerves across the road, there are no cars. She turns from one side to the other: from the fallen gulmohar branches to the manholes covered with fuchsia bougainvillea flowers. Children carrying water bottles around their necks jump on to the sidewalk to avoid her path, and two women in synthetic salwar-kameezes, each on their own phone, hunch their shoulders together, halving their body frames, to squeeze past us.

I try it now, again: release my hands and for an entire hundred metres, I am floating; the wind is in my hair, and it feels cool and light. When I turn to Sam's side of the road, I see Thatha, laughing, his friend laughing too, and when I cycle and come back on another round, he will still be there, and Sam will whoop and clap her hands when I don't fall.

*

3

I am ten minutes late. I arrive at KG Mathias Secondary School (KGM) at 11.10 a.m. Sam insisted on playing pop music early in the morning, while she got ready—all perfect ponytail, just the right amount of hair left out of it, and concealer smudged under her eyes. So I'm already stressed.

So if by the time the bar closes, and you feel like falling down.

There isn't much to say about the place, except looks can be deceptive. The entrance has a cheery blue arch with KG MATHIAS painted on it in white block letters. A wide, sepia dusty field and flat expanses of land, concrete and picture-book square buildings; wooden shutters overlooking the children's playground in the junior block; piles of sand and metal slides dotting the landscape. Behind the red and white awning of the canteen, neem trees canopy the concrete benches on which dried crows' droppings and water stains are chequered, ingrained into the surface. When you were senior enough—class 11 or 12—you could sit on these benches, feeling like you'd entered some secret portal.

I walk towards the library and Michael, the principal's assistant, stops me.

'Excuse me. Ami. Look at the time.'

'What?' I look down at my phone.

'Ten minutes late. You have to get late slip. Go, go.'

'What! I'm not in school any more.'

Michael just frowns at me and waves his register, blue binding and green ruled lines, at me. As far as I know, it's the same register he's had for eleven years.

I'll carry you home.

I walk to the principal's office, get a 'late slip'—a piece of paper with the date, the time and the offender's signature. Michael slips into Sharon's office to get her to sign it. I stand in the waiting room, which is empty. My little column on the late slip reads 'Staff' instead of 'Student'.

Michael slips back into the waiting room.

'Want to go? She is calling.'

I have to put this very delicately without Sharon overhearing. I call Michael to the window. He comes, his arms sagging, eyes flitting away and looking at the sandy field outside. He has no patience for my random questions.

'What you want,' he says.

'Michael. I can't meet her. Please. I have no emotional capacity.'

And you feel like falling down.

Michael scrapes his fingernail on his register. Ajanta Broad Ruled. Digital waterfalls roar on to painted rocks, on the cover. The navy cloth binding is coming loose at the sides.

'If Sharon knows you are here, she will be angry,' Michael says. He scratches the back of his head, eyebrows raised. He clears his throat.

'True,' I say.

He wavers for a moment, his eyes sparkling, then goes back into the principal's office.

'Ah, Ami is gone, ma'am. Class is starting, she has gone,' Michael says.

He blocks me from eyesight, and I walk towards the library, fast, before anyone changes their minds. My feet are hot against the hot concrete, and I fly, rather than walk, across the road, past the canteen, the parked cars, the basketball court, the frangipani trees and hibiscus bushes, back to the library. The sun, golden, ochre, is high in a cloudless sky. Crows chirp on top of the principal's quarters. The shutters above the music room flap in the very still breeze. I step on a half-cracked tamarind shell, sticky fruit peeking through, and a yellowing frangipani petal, before I walk in.

*

4

The library, the arena for my classes, is a two-storey white building with grey stone floors, four-seater tables and shelves and shelves of books. When I was at KGM, I would bunk the Sports Day march-past practice to come here and read books instead.

Quick aside: Is there any point in practising march-past for two months every year? One month in, you are as good as you will ever be in your life. You will also never need this skill again.

'Dude,' Sam says. She is at the library door. 'Only four people are here.'

'That's fine, Sammy.' We must accept my writing class is not Model United Nations. Sam leads the way into the library.

On the ground floor, at wide plywood tables for four, class 12 kids are studying for the SAT. We walk up the stairs to the kiddie section, where the chairs are all colour-checked and tiny. Through the white-painted metal windowpanes, we see the parking lot, the field, rolling like vistas in a painting. The other three are seated—Deeksha, Lavanya and Akshita. It makes sense that these are the people who stayed. Deeksha is Sam's newest friend. Lavanya and Sam have been friends since they were six years old. Akshita and Sam were best friends for years but have recently weathered some turbulent storms.

Lavanya gives me a bony hug and Deeksha smiles at me politely across the table.

'Ami, long time!'

Akshita shuffles up to me while I am pulling out my swivel chair, which has cartoon rabbits peering at me from green, yellow and red squares.

'Ami, hey, I'm joining. That's okay, right?' Akshita asks me in a low voice.

'Yeah, of course.'

She smiles at me in a stiff sort of way and sits across the table, next to Deeksha. From the music room comes the sound of the piano: practice for the carnival, which means hymns all day. The carnival is a major event in KGM and actually in the city. There are red tents on the basketball courts; stalls with popcorn and kathi rolls and pizza slices; and games. All the money goes towards some KGM expense, like the new auditorium. At four in the evening, there are loud choir and student band performances. Everyone comes in groups, pays for overpriced raffle tickets, and stands around just to see who else is there.

Right now, the piano notes are playing out 'How Great Thou Art'.

'Sam, aren't you in the choir?'

'I am,' Sam says. 'I couldn't be in the Annual Day play. Those days are behind me. So I had to do something, otherwise what'll people write in my reference letters.' She shakes her head and smoothes her skirt down as she sits down. Sam has a slightly deeper voice at school, I realize. At home she speaks faster, at a higher pitch. Here, she drawls. I have never seen her in a class, it occurs to me: never like this, pulling at her sleeve, leaning forward, an eyebrow raised. She seems like the whole world could pass her by and she wouldn't even notice: a rayon-clad James Dean.

'Is it okay if you miss practice?' I ask Sam. Piano notes still fill the air, voices slowly joining in.

Then sings my soul.

'Your classes are only once a week. If they're so bad, I'll bunk and go to choir.'

Deeksha shrugs. 'This is way more fun, Ami. We've sung for so many carnivals at this point. Let's try something new.'

This really isn't going to meet that benchmark. I sit down, click my pen on and off. All four of them lean forward and face me.

'So, hi, everyone. I thought I'd try out this writing class, just for the month until school ends. Sam said you might all be interested.'

'Of course we're interested,' Deeksha says.

Good start. I look at the midnight-blue *ISC Whispers of Poesy* textbook on the table. 'I'm going to use the school poetry book, okay? Try and make it fun.'

'Let's see if that's possible,' Sam says. She gestures to Deeksha. 'By the way, Deeksha is in charge of our Literary Society.'

'Which we haven't done anything with yet,' Deeksha said. 'Maybe I'll learn from you, Ami.'

'Ami's great at writing,' Sam says.

'I'm not,' I say automatically, a reflex, like 'Bless you' when someone sneezes.

'You are,' Lavanya says. 'I've read literally everything you wrote in the *KGM Digest*. They were really good. Sam, you use Ami's notes only, no? For *Macbeth*?' She turns to me. Her eyes are so pale, they are basically transparent. Every movement of hers is slow, deliberate, viewed through frosted glass.

Deeksha clears her throat. 'So, Ami, we've only met a few times before you left school. And yeah, of course I've read your essays in the *KGM Digest*, I always skipped to your grade and read your stuff. I'm not really a writer, but I feel like this can help me lead the Lit Soc and maybe tap further into my feelings, emotions and all that fun stuff.'

'Ami, how come you're back now?' Akshita jumps in. She is a walking-talking italics font—leaning forward, asking a question before even having spoken, loosely plaited hair, electric-current eyes and movements. Something is edgy about her—literally.

The others all look at their nails, avoiding eye contact.

'Uh.' I scramble for the word. I have a sharp, perky answer all ready in my head and then the words get lodged, like seeds, in my throat.

'We don't need to talk about that,' Deeksha chips in for me. 'I'm just glad you're here.' She smiles.

'Of course we need to talk about it,' Akshita insists. 'Sam was saying we should come for this class and Ami needs help and now she's back home and all, we should know what happened, no?'

I would answer if I had to, just make up something as usual, but I don't have to. The rest of the girls seem to have adopted me as a cause.

Sam swivels her chair towards Akshita. 'I didn't say that, bro.' The 'bro' sounds quite ominous.

'Akshita.' It's Lavanya. 'Come on, you can't talk like that.'

'She didn't mean anything, Ami, don't worry.' Deeksha tries to smile lightly.

The whispers are getting fierce—still at library-mandated volume but in fast, hissing voices.

'Dude, this class is about writing, not all this stuff,' Deeksha says. 'And I know it's not like everyone's thing. We're starting slow. So if you don't want to stay . . .'

There is a second of silence, and then Akshita stands up, creaks her chair wheels, picks up her hair scrunchie and notebook labelled 'KGM Rough Work Scribbler' and walks out of the library. No more scribblings for her. We sit there, letting the ripples settle.

'Sorry, Ami,' Sam says. Her eyes have gone wide and her voice low.

'Akshita's just . . . been like this for some time,' Lavanya tells me, with the voice of a surgeon on *Grey's Anatomy* talking to a patient's family. 'We weren't sure whether to call her . . . She said she wanted to come . . .'

Sit down, we have to inform the family. We tried everything we could.

'Sam, you should really tell Sharon,' Deeksha says. Sam shakes her head.

'Let's talk about something else,' Sam says. Her smile is slightly forced. She takes off the cap of her pen. 'So, Ami,' she says. 'What should we do for Thursday?'

A beat, and then I tune into Sam's frequency and speak in a determined, normal voice, too. 'Okay, so. For today, shall

 we just each write about something that's bothering us? Then next time, we can figure out how to address that through all the poems we'll study.'

'Bothers us about our writing or just life?' Deeksha asks.

'Just in general.'

Deeksha, Lavanya and Sam lean back in their seats, writing things down.

I see, as though it's happening at just the next table, Thatha awake early morning, sitting at his desk and writing. Me writing in a little Classmate notebook, too, copying him. He wrote in tiny scrawls, and I followed the curve of the Tamil letters: his spilling looping letters and my boxy cursive ones.

'Thatha. Is this correct?'

'You keep on writing, don't be shy!'

Lavanya stops writing and looks up.

'Ey, why, why did you ask Akshita to come?' she asks Sam.

Sam's chair squeaks. 'Listen, I didn't know she'd be annoying. She's known Ami for years. I thought she'd want to come.'

'I knew you shouldn't have called her,' Lavanya says.

Sam picks up her pen. 'Guys, can we just work?'

Deeksha and Lavanya look at each other but drop whatever it is they really wanted to discuss. I decide to give them time to write, and go downstairs to borrow a book using Sam's library card. I wander around the shelves, the lovely smell of yellow pages and half-torn plastic covers in the air, and I find *Tuesdays with Morrie*, which I'd first read in this exact library. I borrow it, sit down and read.

* * *

After the class, Sam and I walk out, down the stone path, past the parking lot. We reach the bushes cropped into a square, short line. They border a pathway leading to the old principal's building, which houses the music room, the book room and the Lost and Found. The choir is currently singing 'O Come, All Ye Faithful.'

'Now, at least, should you go join practice?' I ask Sam.

Sam is playing with the top of the bushes, the sharp, waxy leaves.

'I'll go in two minutes.'

There's clearly something more she wants to say, but one cannot push Sam. She is swaying from side to side a little, subconsciously. All her weight on her left foot, then her right. I copy her, and she frowns at me.

'What are you doing?'

I laugh. 'Want to eat cake?'

'No. Pizza.'

Sam shuffle runs and I slow walk to the canteen and we stand in line. There are just two people ahead of us. The canteen keeper is on leave, so Michael is here, in charge. He's talking in a staccato voice and somehow both putting money into the plastic box and giving people apple juice, chips and cake at the same time. He widens his eyes when he sees me.

'Here also you've come,' Michael says, by way of greeting.

'How's life, Michael? Egg puff and veg pizza,' I say.

Michael places the egg puff and pizza on thin, oil-covered tissues on the counter and smiles and shakes his head at me.

Sam takes the food and we sit down on the covered-up water well next to the canteen. Tall trees—copper pod, neem, cotton—

sway above us. Sam eats her puff and gives me the pizza. After a few bites, we switch and I get the puff.

'What are you thinking?' Sam asks.

'You'll say I'm being depressing.'

'Tell me.' Sam buzzes.

I feel a salty electric feeling in my jaw and my cheeks, which is that classic pre-cry feeling. I am thinking about how the worst torture had occurred when I was in KGM and I thought it would stop with me. I didn't know it would mutate and affect Sam's batch. Affect Sam.

'Rohan,' I say. The perfect metaphor for this torture I am talking about: Rohan Mathew.

'That drug addict from your class?'

I shrug. I feel tears rise and fall, on to my tissue. 'Alcoholism was the only proven charge,' I say.

'You know, he's going bald now?' Sam asks and looks at me closely. 'My God, Ami. You're actually crying!'

The world glimmers. My under-eyes turn warm. I look out, past the gate. I see the two-floor boxy bungalows, all converted now: a tuition centre, a driving school, an architect's office. Wet, white towels, now pale blue, hang on the clothes lines, swaying, tangling up with electricity cables, paper flyers for JEE coaching and wide, fat almond leaves at the tops of trees.

I try to focus on the almond leaves and not my tears.

I hate, so much, that I cannot change things that have happened, in the way that they have happened, and that they can crop up any time, plastic bags washed on to the beach, and remind me of everything I'm trying not to remember.

'Ami . . .'

'Stop it. Otherwise I won't give you my puff.'

'You have some left?' Sam asks.

'One bite.'

'Givegivegivegive!'

*

5

To explain, in 500 words or under:

In class 3, Rohan was all long-nose, short-syllabled, always present in everyone's minds. He was every girl's answer to 'Who do you *liiike*—in *that* way?', but it didn't really mean anything. It was hardly a Roland Barthes-level conception of love.

He lived in Kotturpuram, near the crèches and the matriculation school. He would come over often, and we'd play with mud in the garden, making little huts or snowballs. We were eight. Even though the food in my house wasn't fancy like his, he never thought he was too good for me. We didn't have pastas or salads or quiches. We had sambar and beans curry, or bread and pickle, or Britannia sliced cheese. We would swing back and forth on the front gate, trying to get large nuts to fall off the tree, using the watchman's long stick.

By the time class 6 rolled around, my 'best friend', Malvika Rao, had decided that Rohan would talk to no one but her. One day, at our friend Akshara's house (back then, every girl was friends with every other girl), we were all playing Lock and Key. Like deer who seek higher ground before high tide, I felt like something terrible would happen. Instead of doing something, I just moved into the dining room when it was my turn to catch. Everyone else spread out across Akshara's apartment. Malvika and Rohan stood in one corner of Akshara's room.

The hall was beautiful. It had a big wooden dining table; a wall decorated with Turkish blue plates. Another wall, painted banana yellow, was filled with frames of KGM class photos, from class 2 to present. Woody, the beagle, was sleeping under the table.

Stay here, I told myself. *Just trust me.*

But I didn't trust myself. Someone yelled 'ten'—I'd forgotten to count—and then I ran into Akshara's room. I felt the drawstring on my newly bought, uncomfortable cargo pants come loose.

(I made Amma take me shopping and I bought them just for this party. Is that ironic? Maybe. It's definitely not joyful.)

For a brief moment, the pants slipped down.

I retied them, but the smell of plastic and bitter blood filled the room. I had my period and hadn't yet mastered pad-placement. For one moment, total silence: just the sound of Woody's breathing in the house. Then—one second later—I thought, *maybe nobody saw me.*

Everything was quiet. But then, the edge of the room started shaking. Malvika and Rohan laughed and laughed, looking at each other, their shoulders shaking softly and their eyes preoccupied, like I didn't exist. Again, hardly Barthes, but I didn't know that then.

I walked back outside. The sea breeze was hot, laden with humidity as it blew through the window.

On the wall I saw small circles of my face, from class 2, class 3, class 4, peering down at me. Two ponytails, bangs, hair falling straight to my ears. I stayed very still, frowning, so as not to cry.

(This predated my crying-in-public days.) I just focused on the time. Amma was going to pick me up at six. It was five. How time seemed to expand in the world outside, but stayed still inside, like a sleeping beagle.

Akshara and Malvika walked into the room and sat on the bench next to me.

You're the one who wanted to invite him, Malvika said. *So desperate.*

I moved a centimetre away, looking up at my own face on the wall. I heard Woody breathing and just could not fathom what to do or say, how to feel.

Somebody tell me something.

Tell me how to feel.

In the corridors of KGM, whenever I passed by Malvika or Rohan, I moved all the way to the other side, and a crowd of people came between us, separated us. I looked away. Like we were the survivors of a horrific car crash that nobody else knew about. And we never wanted to tell ourselves again.

*

6

Writing draft/Notes about Thatha: 7 November 2013

In those days, I went back home exhausted and tired every day. One day, I got home with a headache ringing through my entire body. I went to our room, past the chart-paper sign, sellotaped to our door, which read: 'AMRITA AND SAMITA SHEKAR'S ROOM DO NOT ENTER!' in bright red and blue and yellow. Sam had laid out all her dolls on my bed, neatly—the dolls on their way to eat their little plastic food, the blue plastic table laid with a perennial eggs breakfast.

'Sam, move this stuff,' I said. She had changed from her uniform into a red T-shirt, but still wore the KGM blue shorts. She was sitting at our desk and playing on our yellow Casio keyboard, banging away songs and changing the 'voice' to keyboards, trumpets, honky-tonk piano.

'Sam.'

She grinned up at me from the chair—it was too big for her, and she had her legs up on the seat.

'Sam,' I said. 'Move your stuff.'

'You wrote in my diary on every page. I can't keep my stuff on your bed?' She was all bright eyes, sharp elbows, quick-moving jumps. She jumped out of the chair and on to her bed, dancing along to the keyboard's jivey piano and trumpets melody.

'Sam, I'm serious, move it.' I pulled her arm so that she would listen.

'You move it!'

'Oh my God.' I swept her toys off the bed, and one tiny purple boot fell near the desk, one tiny doll in a blue dress fell below the bed, and the tables clattered on to the floor. It looked like an earthquake had hit a little toy town.

Sam gasped, a tiny sound over the trumpets, and then she ran into the cupboard and pulled out her notebook in which I'd scribbled AMI SHEKAR AMI SHEKAR AMI SHEKAR in red crayon on every page, and she held it open right in front of my face. 'See! And I didn't say anything!'

She sat down on her bed and unplugged the Casio keyboard. There was silence in the room.

I sat down in the corner of my now-empty bed, leaning against the wall.

'Ami, you have become *so mean* these days,' Sam said.

I didn't say anything, sitting there in my sweltering school uniform (why rayon in summer, why). The fan creaked on the ceiling. The plastic wire of the keyboard rattled on the floor. My name stared back at me, in my confident letters, from the blue-lined pages of Sam's notebook.

Thatha walked into the room. He had just woken up—his hair was rumpled and his vest sagged, faded from a hundred washes, the neckline loose and almost reaching his sternum. His pink towel was thrown over his shoulder.

'*Aiyyy*,' he said. '*Enna di*. What is all this?' He neatly picked his way through the plastic toys, a real-life game of Minesweeper, and sat down on my bed. He lifted up the pillow from below my arm and placed it vertically against the wall. He folded it down and leaned against it.

Oh, no, I thought. *My pillow.* The thought was niggling but distant, like it wasn't even me thinking it but somebody else.

'What is the problem, Ami,' Thatha asked. 'Sam wanted to play with you, that is all.'

*

7

It's ten minutes into the writing class on Day Two, and Sam shuffles into the room.

'Football,' Sam says to me, to explain her shirt and her lateness. Her light blue shirt has turned dark blue with sweat. The sweat vaguely forms the shape of the Caspian Sea on her back.

It's a bright day. The sun hangs high in the sky. Sweat spreads across my back like a second skin.

There are sponge cakes from the canteen in the middle of the library table. Deeksha has surrounded the cakes with books and pens.

'Where's Lavanya?' Sam asks.

'She should be here,' Deeksha says.

I consider addressing the issue of the empty chair—Akshita isn't in the room either. But since the other two are just eating cake, I only address the issue of the cake.

'I thought food wasn't allowed inside the library?'

Deeksha shrugs. 'So we'll eat them fast.'

We settle down. Sam and Deeksha look at me as they eat. 'Let's start, Ami,' Deeksha says. 'It's almost 3.15.'

'Okay, so, things that bother us . . .' I start. 'Deeksha?'

'Okay,' Deeksha says and shakes her head. She smoothens down her shirt and sits straighter. 'So, for me, the one thing that really bothers me is whenever people aren't listening to me. I feel like I have to try so hard, but people still don't really listen, if you know what I mean—like really listen. I feel the need to be louder than other people.'

This entire speech has been said like she's afraid time will run out: 'needtobeLOUDERthan . . .' She clicks her tongue and waves her hands. 'I mean, just a metaphor.'

Sam pulls out a folded piece of paper. 'I actually wrote something,' she starts. 'I can't just talk on the spot and all, like Deeksha. She can do that any time.'

'That's not true, Sam,' Deeksha says, tilting towards her like a leaf to the sun. She kicks her under the table lightly. How is Deeksha's ponytail so perfectly smooth, falling so thin and straight? Lavanya walks in silently. I only realize she is in the room when she pulls out the chair right next to me.

'Sorry, sorry, I got late.'

'No problem,' I say.

We look at the seat to Lavanya's right—still empty. We all turn back to each other.

The fan fills the room with a soft rhythm, cool and warm on my arm, in turns. I tap my nail on the table.

'I was just telling Deeksha, I wrote my speech down, about what bothers me, unlike her. Remember her vice-captain speech?' Sam asks Lavanya.

'You were so good, Deeksha. Your speech was easily the best, even though you made it up on the spot.' Lavanya nods. 'Hey, even I wrote something for today.' She opens her notebook. 'A poem for today's class.'

'Wowwww,' says Deeksha.

'Thought may as well embrace this full Lit Soc thing, right,' Lavanya says, and laughs, more air than voice: a half-sound like she can't break the silence.

'Read it, bro,' Sam nudges her.

Lavanya clears her throat, sits up straight. The beginnings of a ceremony. She reads aloud:

Perfect Skin
My skin is just my skin,
Sometimes too pale, too big
It's a blanket covering too much,
Not enough, all the lumps, all the folds

Lavanya's eyes are on her piece of paper, but she raises her gaze slightly; she notices everyone looking at her. She looks down again and takes a deep breath.

Sometimes it asks me questions.
Is this too much?
Too little?
What will they think?
Do they like what they see?
I wish my skin was perfect
Because it is skin.
Not because it's pale and thin.

There is a short pause, the pause before the beat drops in a song. Then Sam exhales. 'That was lovely,' she says.

'Really good, Lavanya.' I nod. It's like the writing in the *KGM Digest*—it's holding something back, but there's so much that glimmers through the lines. As though accidentally, hiding just enough, Lavanya revealed what worries her. Her body, skin, how others see her . . . All those thoughts lie right underneath, and we see only what she finally says aloud: we see only the fields that the windows of the train show us, before we pass them by.

'Your turn, Ami,' Sam says. 'Go, go.'

'No, you go, Sam.'

'No. *You.*'

I look around at the small library room we are sitting in, and then at Sam's face. She is buttoning and unbuttoning the top button of her shirt, and her eyes are focused, bright.

There is a light dusting of a frown on her forehead. She means business. I remember standing in the corner of the room during her birthday parties, handing out return gifts to her friends.

'Time,' I say, my words a cliché before I have spoken. The library chair squeaks against the grey mosaic floor, the smooth tile flecked with cream, black and yellow. I place my hands under my thighs and they stay nice, warm, numb from my weight, pins and needles slowly forming. I lean forward. Clifford the Big Red Dog smiles at me from a framed painting in the corner.

'I feel bad that time keeps passing and I can't really do anything about it. Logically, I know it's not faster or slower than normal. But I have trouble remembering that.'

They nod their heads slowly, and Sam tilts her head. It's like they're tarot card readers. Deeksha looks at me as though she's trying to X-ray my brain, understand what I'm really trying to say. We have to understand everything through this semi-formal relationship, look for what's hidden. Lavanya is looking at the poetry textbook.

'Like the dancers on Keats' Grecian urn,' Lavanya says. 'Right?'

For ever panting, and for ever young.

'Brilliant, exactly, look at "Ode on a Grecian Urn",' I say. 'It's the same thing. Keats obviously puts it much better than I did. Keats has his urn. He wants things to always stay the same. Life doesn't work like that. We see how he feels, how he really wants that sense of permanence.' I wonder if I've talked too long, but the girls are still looking at me with their heads cocked and those unbroken waves between us.

Therefore, ye soft pipes, play on.

'Why do they make such cool poems so boring in school? This one could be so interesting, but then they add all these workbook questions and you have to sit there underlining each word and writing its meaning,' Lavanya says.

She plays with her pen. The sides of her fingers are stained royal blue, the diamond-grip of the pen leaving diamond-shaped indents near her nails.

'Let's do some object poetry,' I say. 'Shall we write rough notes on what the object could be and what it means to you? Like, for example, I talked about time passing. The object I'm thinking of is a yellow Casio keyboard, which Sam and I used to play when we were younger. We would play tunes and dance around. It's a feeling from my past.'

They all begin scribbling in their notebooks, and I open the textbook and reread Keats' poems as they write. It's like I can feel exactly what Keats meant. The air from the fan tickles the hairs on my neck.

42

Thou canst not leave thy song, nor ever can those trees be bare.

At the end of the hour, everyone looks at each other and stretches. Deeksha switches off the light and fan, and the sunlight suddenly seems stark outside through the pale window grilles.

We walk downstairs and part ways. Sam and I walk past the library teacher, whom we all slightly raise our eyebrows at, to say hello, and we pass by the 'senior' bookshelves and larger tables.

In the parking lot outside, we stretch again and our arms crack from disuse. Sam blinks her eyes. The whole school is spread out before us, practically empty except for a few dots here and there. Sam crosses her legs and looks at her watch.

'I have choir practice in five minutes,' she says.

'So let's stay here for four minutes,' I say.

We lean against the library wall, lounging, and I close my eyes against the sun. It's pale now, hidden behind a cloud. A temporary lull.

'Hey, Sammy, you never read your poem.'

'Oh true. But *technically*, it's not a poem. It's a note or a thought.' She looks down at her crumpled piece of paper. 'You won't mind?'

'Why will I mind?'

'I don't know . . . you shouldn't overanalyse it, Ami.'

'I won't.'

'Okay.' Sam takes a deep breath and unfolds her piece of paper. She reads in a low voice, as the music room plays piano notes from choir practice in the background:

'I wake up with this feeling sometimes. Not like a recurring dream because nobody has those in real life, but just a feeling when I open my eyes in the morning. It's like I'm the only person standing and everybody else is lying on the ground, asleep or unconscious, and nobody is around to help me. And nobody is listening. It's just me. I have to save everybody, wake them up, save the planet all by myself.'

She stops reading, folds the paper up into a tiny square— its phantom spiral holes poking out, its ink bleeding on to its blue lines—and puts it back into her pocket, brushes down her skirt and then looks up.

I feel a wringing inside me, a sudden softening as if all my joints have melted and are replaced by water.

'I know,' Sam says. 'It's actually good that I didn't read it out in front of everyone. It's so dramatic.'

I quickly compose myself. Sam puts her hand on top of mine: warm-sweet-sweaty.

'Come on, Sammy,' I say. 'You're not that deep. You just read a Danielle Steel book.'

She looks at me for a second, frowning. I can almost hear her thinking, *should I laugh or not?* Then she laughs.

Her shoulders crumple up. And her shirt is suddenly baggy on her.

'Excuse me, what's wrong with that? Her novels are emotional journeys!'

*

8

Stop crying your heart out, Oasis tells me. I am tired down to my bones, and I'm dusting my books with an old T-shirt-turned-rag. The shelves have grown dusty, and the books are slightly waterlogged, curled and bumpy despite sitting indoors for months.

Why're you scared? Oasis asks.

I decide to attempt my history essay once again.

This was one of the last essays I wrote in college before coming home. I failed the class. I couldn't pay attention in history classes even though they were my favourite. But I am still smart or at least, no less smart than I used to be. So I'm not sure what happened.

How are issues of modernity and reform treated in twentieth-century Indian literature? Your answer should refer to two writers or works from the module.

Sam flits into my room like a firefly. 'Can I borrow something?'

'What?'

'Something. I need something nice to wear for Deeksha's birthday and I'm bored of all my clothes.' She lingers at the edge of the room, the door half-open, and Amma's voice wafts in, light and lilting, floating towards the ceiling. 'Ami, come to the hall for one minute.'

Sam doesn't move (she was not called) and neither do I (bone-heavy tiredness). Sam just leans against the doorpost, frowning.

'Ami. Come here one second,' Amma says.

I slide out past Sam and go downstairs.

'Ami, I spoke to Nirmal. I called her,' Amma says, as I walk into the living room. Appa is sitting hunched on the sofa, sipping his drink.

'She says we should do some tests and all. She said to go to Ignatius Hospital, get these tests done, then go meet her. I'll call, make the appointment.'

'Psychiatrist?' Appa asks. 'Why?'

I really, really, do not want to be having this conversation. Amma is perfectly calm and measured, but I know the other two people in the room will not be. I am a ticking metronome and Appa is crashing cymbals.

'Um,' I say.

'Don't say "um",' Appa says before I even get the word out.

'Shekar . . .' Amma says automatically, like swatting a fly. The doorbell rings.

Appa goes to get the door and is joined by Sam, who clatters down the stairs in my grey top. It's slightly loose on her gangly, scarecrow-like frame but otherwise gorgeous, bringing out every hint of glimmer on her face. Appa opens the door. Siddharth Agarwal stands in the doorway, his face framed by the indigo evening sky.

'Hey,' he says. 'Hi, Uncle.' Then he waves in our general direction. He is taller than I remember from even just a few months ago, but he otherwise looks the same: a stretched version of an old photograph of Sam and her friends.

'Hey, Siddharth, how's it going?' Appa booms. His voice ricochets off the small foyer walls.

'Good, Uncle.'

'Good, good.'

Siddharth is in rowing whites. Down our road is the rowing club. Apparently, the river is filled with so much heavy mud, sewage and sludge that when rowers fall in, it takes hours to pull them out. Once, a rower fell in and nobody could pull him out; there was too much sludge. He forgot to hold on to the boat. He may or may not have made it out alive. Retellings end differently depending on how generous or morbid the teller is feeling that day.

'Bye, Pa.' Sam waves.

Before she goes, Sam widens her eyes at me, sending me a silent message. *Will you be okay?*

I nod, moving my chin and head just enough so that she can see, but not so much that Appa or Siddharth will notice.

We are like gangsters in an Italian mobster's villa. Then Sam holds up her phone, sending me another silent message: *Text me if you need anything.*

I tap my phone in response.

Back in the hall, Appa takes a sip of his drink.

'She doesn't need all this psychiatrist and all,' Appa says to Amma. 'Let her just relax, take some rest. *Avlo dhaan.* Then she can go back in January. She'll just graduate late. But many people just graduate in winter instead of summer, no? Ami?'

I am trying not to be difficult (Appa's word, not mine), but I feel unable to say more than a few words without crying. Which I feel would significantly undermine my negotiating position. My phone gleams in the yellow lamplight (Amma has more lamps in the room than actual lights). *Should I text Sam?* I should give it some time before stressing her out. She probably hasn't even reached the gate yet.

'Ami.' Appa sips his drink, ice clattering against ice. 'I'm talking to you.'

'Oh . . . yeah . . .' I start. I turn to Amma. 'Nothing, Ma, the dean said if I go back in Jan but take summer classes, I can graduate at the same time as normal, in two years. I can just graduate late, in the October ceremony instead of June,' I say.

'See,' Appa says and leans back. He's declared order in court. 'See, better to say "Okay, whatever has happened now, leave it." But she can start slowly in January, no? Then she'll graduate in October, it's a proper ceremony, no, Ami? See Hema, other PhD students or late students or whatever will graduate. Why can't she do that? Why can't she send Mallory that email?'

'But that has nothing to do with this, Shekar. You also know that. Ami also agreed to go to Nirmal, didn't you, Ami? Now why are you both objecting?'

'But why, there must be a reason, no?' Appa looks at me.

'That's why we're going to the doctor, to find out. Shekar, you're not making sense,' Amma says. She takes a sip of her drink, leans against the sofa and rests her head on her hand. She looks through me, lost in thought. She shakes her glass and then holds it out to me. 'Get me ice, no.'

I take her glass and walk into the kitchen, the tiles cool on my feet. The room smells like fresh kozhumbu and boiled rice. A bowl of green-orange oranges lies covered with a cloth; some weak, anaemic flies buzz around it. Remnants of Amma's peanut salad lie on a cutting board: onion peel, half-squeezed lemon, knife, coriander. I hear Amma and Appa's murmuring voices as I enter again.

'Ah, so, Ami. You're not feeling sick, no fever, pain, no symptoms, correct?' Appa starts again.

'Nothing like that. I've just been feeling weird,' I say.

'What is "weird"?' Appa regards me through the prism of his glass.

'She's going through a difficult time, ma,' Amma says. 'That's why we let her come home.'

'Ma, come on,' I say. *Please drop the topic, please.* Like in a thermometer, I can feel my tension rise and rise and rise. How high can the mercury rise before the glass breaks?

'Let her tell me, Hema,' Appa says. 'You keep saying something happened, something happened. But what happened, that's what I'm trying to understand,' Appa says.

I have to speak now. Nowhere else to go. 'Appa, I don't know how to describe it. I just feel like something's wrong. I feel hopeless and I feel like I can't handle anything.'

'Nobody wants to handle anything. Obviously nobody wants to. But we have to do it, that's all. It's part of life. Look at all of us. We're handling things, no? Everyone is handling things.'

Amma has had enough of this conversation. 'I'll make the appointment,' she says.

'You don't need to come, Ma. I'll go myself,' I say.

'Of course I'm coming,' Amma says, at the same time as Appa talks: 'Nobody needs to go!'

*

9

Amma is already in the car. It's the day of my hospital visit and I'm late. Sam follows me out through the door.

'Good luck,' she says. 'Here.' She gives me five pistas and munches on the rest herself. Her feet are bare as she walks with me to the car park and then runs back inside the house.

Amma is wearing a white kurta, her hair is freshly washed, and she has dark eyeliner on. She looks bright, alive, the exact opposite of me. I'm wearing a kurta and tights and my hair is in a braid, but it just looks wrong. I look the way smokers' nails look—ashy grey and faded. Or like the destroyed grey lungs on cigarette packets. If someone took a photograph of this moment, I'd look back and wonder, *Why did my face and skin look like that? Was it just that day or was it all year?*

We start driving on to the main road when I feel those little electric ants come back—in my hands, inside my head, down my neck and shoulders. I feel the first of the tears fall. My shoulders start shaking and my face is warm, my vision is blurry and my head is filled with ocean rocks.

Amma turns to look at me, while she drives. '*Enna ma achu*? Should I stop the car?'

I shake my head. 'Sorry, Ma.'

'What "sorry"?' She leans over and wipes my face roughly, while still looking at the road. The Cars are singing.

Who's gonna drive you home tonight?

'Come on, you choose some music,' Amma says.

'I don't mind your songs, Ma.'

'Come on. My treat. Play your favourite whiny music.'

I try to smile. I hope Amma sees my smile. I try to perk myself up, push myself up by my elbows until I am sitting straight. 'Should I pick a sad song?'

'Whatever you want.'

I pick 'Valium Skies' by The Verve.

How do you keep yourself from folding?

I lean my head against the window: we are flying, coasting, and the tall trees, the gated houses, the biryani centres, the provision stores with tea stalls under their awnings pass in a blur of blue and yellow.

My breaths come through ragged, sharp branches in my chest cavity. Time passes in long, aching drips, half in a dream, and then we are at a crossroads, blue signposts hanging as if from the sky. Every place is indicated with an arrow, compressing distance: as if T. Nagar, Anna Nagar, Parrys, all lie right ahead, just there.

Amma turns to look at me. 'We're here.'

We walk into the hospital, past the ramp with two ambulances, two security guards and a stretcher. The lobby and the corridors all smell vaguely like plastic. We get into the lift and press 2. Then we have to squeeze right into the back, because an empty stretcher is wheeled in by an attendant in white. The stretcher smells of chemical metal and sweet (too sweet), crisp white sheets.

Seems like the whole world is losing.

On the second floor, we walk along a tight corridor and try not to breathe in the smell of the IV drips. Two receptionists talk to each other behind their counters, clacking at their computers, though I am standing right there. One receptionist looks at me, then right back at her colleague.

'Hi,' I say.

She keeps clacking on her keyboard and adjusts the bobby pin in her hair.

Amma taps on the counter loudly. 'Excuse me, madam.'

The woman with the bobby pin looks up. 'Yes, madam, tell.'

'I'm here to see the psychologist,' I say. 'Dr Yogita.'

She looks at her phone and plays with her fading pink nail polish and bites her lip in a distracted way. 'Reference?'

'Dr Nirmal Sharma, psychiatrist.'

'Show your prescription, madam.' So Amma obliges. She shows her a digital prescription, blurry except for the test names, like codes, at the bottom. In royal blue. The doctor's stamp on the page is fading at the corners.

'Wait here, the test will take two hours,' she says. 'Minimum.'

'What's the maximum?' I look up at her.

She ignores me and gets up to go call the doctor. I turn to Amma and widen my eyes and she squeezes my hand. Just beyond Amma I can see donation boxes for medical camps; a weighing scale; a diagram of the human body.

The psychologist shows up, pale brown hair, pale green kurta, flustered eyes. 'Ami?'

'Yes.'

'I'm Dr Yogita. Do you want to come with me? So, it's a two-hour test, is that okay? You can pay at the end.'

'Sure.'

'It's in room 221. Just this way.'

I turn to Amma again. 'I'll wait downstairs,' she says. 'Message me.'

'Ma, they said two hours . . .'

'I'll wait. Go, go.'

Dr Yogita does all the tests Nirmal had asked for: various types of descriptions and self-analysis and assignments. *What do these shapes mean? Rank this statement from one to four.* Her assistant, who looks as old as me, walks in to lead me to another free room for the next test. She plugs in a laptop, explains the instructions of the personality test and leaves me alone after telling me to save the results. 'It's really important to save the page,' she says, as if I am the one controlling things here. 'Okay?'

'Okay.'

I sit there, on the patient's side of the table, alone except for a box of tissues, a silver pen stand, a white curtain blocking off an examination bed and a rather depressing painting that some children have made for a Dr Kinnari in bright red finger paint. It reads, 'THANK YOU, DOCTOR. LOTS OF LOVE. THANK YOU.' Tiny red smiley faces line the piece of paper and they have even painted the hospital logo: two open hands with a floating heart balancing on them. The painting is framed. I wonder if the two children, Advik and Ritika, are still in the hospital. I try to focus on the test and press *next* and *next* and *next*. My fingers cramp from scrolling through the deepest recesses of my personality.

Two hours later, the assistant, slightly red in the face, opens the door. She is fifteen minutes late. She arrives just at the point when I wonder what happens if nobody collects this laptop and how much it costs to do this whole thing again. Who will I have to call to fix up all those appointments? What if I never find my way downstairs?

'All finished?' she asks. 'Great.'

Is it? I am guessing she is a clinical psychology student, and if I were her, I would be so excited to help patients out. I wouldn't be in such a hurry to move on to the next thing. At least, I'd ask if they were comfortable, did they want water.

I pay at the reception and follow Amma's texts to the hospital café on the ground floor. I take the stairs to avoid being trapped with any morbid empty stretchers. In the small café filled with the smells of burnt sambar and stale sandwiches, I spot Amma sitting with a cup of lemon tea and a cookie, reading on her iPad. She is surrounded by people and tables with crunched-up tissues and styrofoam cups. Every table is sticky or wet with something or other. I look at Amma, lines under her eyes, eating the cookie. I take in the scene for a few moments, a few great moments, because in these moments I haven't ruined the peace of the scene— smudged fingers on oil paint that hasn't dried. I walk up to her.

'Hi, Ma.'

She looks up and reaches out her hand, closing her iPad. 'All done?'

'Done.'

'Paid?'

'Paid. Sorry you had to wait.'

'How was it?'

'Horrible. Long. Sorry it was so long.'

'*Chi*, why are you saying sorry. This is fine.'

'This is not fine.'

I look around. At the table behind me, another woman and her daughter are stirring their tea, milk floating on the top, silently.

'Next time, I'll go alone, okay?'

'Ami . . .'

'Just agree.'

'Can you please sit down for two minutes?'

I sit. Amma takes a sip of her lemon tea.

'How bad is it?' I ask, looking at the amber liquid. Little tea leaves float on top.

'Here, take a sip. Not bad.'

'You're such a liar.'

Amma smiles at me, over her cup. 'Don't worry. It'll be good to meet Nirmal. She helped Thatha a lot.'

'Thatha saw a psychiatrist?'

'The psychiatrist saw Thatha.' She laughs. 'Nirmal came home.'

'Really? When . . .?' I'm going through the Jenga blocks in my mind, trying to place this new information.

'When Thatha came back from the hospital, I thought he might have depression. So I said, "Nirmal, just come home and see." She was supposed to be really good, I heard she actually listens to patients. You remember that Jogesh, that

58

Cognizant guy I used to do coaching for? He recommended her, just gave me her card and I called. He said "The wait is long but just go to her, nobody else, don't bother with other psychiatrists." I just called. She came right away. I had to do something. Thatha was just so slow after the surgery. You were there when she came home, or maybe you were in school or piano class. Something. I don't remember.'

'Ma, why did you never tell me?'

'What's there to tell?' Amma leans back, reties her hair. The strands near her temple are tugged upwards and pull her forehead back. 'He gave up on life. All those chemicals got to him and he had so much pain with his hip. I finally said, "Enough, I'm calling Nirmal." Appa kept saying, "My father, I'll decide." I said, "By the time you decide, he would have suffered so much. So I'm sorry, I'm not going to wait."'

I feel the sharpness of my bones on the chair.

'I could make out, you know, that something was wrong. I saw it in Thatha's eyes. He had just stopped caring. More than usual. As it is, he was a little detached. He once told me he can't take care of you girls every day and he was finished with his parenting days.'

'He said that?'

'Don't take it personally, Ami, it's not a bad thing. People just say such things sometimes without thinking. It doesn't mean they don't care. I would ask him also, "How are you, Maama," and he would say, "Just as I was yesterday, and tomorrow, I will be just as I am today." But this time was different. After he came back from the hospital, he was different. I could just see it. He didn't care whether he took his medicine or whether he remembered me. He just didn't care any more. It just became too much for him, that's all.'

I tread carefully—if I speak too much, it might startle Amma and she will retreat. I fold the bottom of my shirt into accordion pleats and try to stay absolutely still.

I can picture Thatha, leaning back on his bed, his eyes closed, the room smelling of floor cleaner and bandages. I can almost see his sharp elbows.

I've moved and I see Amma look at me—her eyes are big and deep and chocolate-brown. She stretches, and takes a deep breath in. The moment is still there, alive, breathing, slowly. It hasn't been poked or punctured. It hasn't died.

'I was right here in this hospital,' Amma says. 'We looked at him through the small window of the ICU. We saw when his heart stopped beating.' Amma taps on the table.

She inhales. She splays her arms on the two chairs on either side of her, like she needs the support. But her eyes don't betray any emotion. They will close up again, soon.

An ambulance siren wails, followed by three car honks, evenly apart and then altogether like a rainstorm. Amma turns around and throws her teacup into the green dustbin, stained with brown splatters.

The moment is gone.

'Shall we go?' Amma asks.

I picture Thatha sitting on the chair outside the house, his eyes closely following me as I walked back from school.

'Let's go,' I say.

*

10

Writing draft/Notes about Thatha: 15 November 2013

On one of the last days of August, Thatha was lying in his bed. It had rained, and the sky was clear, empty and grey.

I crouched near the staircase. I could smell Dettol and disinfectant from Thatha's room, but I was too scared to go in.

I heard the clack of Thatha's walker. The room was quiet—no wails or screams from Thatha, which normally shook the walls and filled every particle of air.

So I walked downstairs, still in my school uniform—skirt askew, shirt turned stiff with sweat. Prickly heat on my neck.

Thatha was standing at the door, bent over his walker, all shoulder-bone and twig-arm, hair slightly ruffled, loose vest—but still looking like Thatha.

'See, I took a step,' Thatha said. 'I took two steps. Three steps.'

'So you can walk again!' I smiled.

'Yes, seems to be.' He looked up at me suddenly. 'You know my father is visiting?'

'What?'

'Yes, yes, he's coming from Japan.' Thatha nodded.

Thatha's father died years ago and had definitely never been to Japan. So who was he talking about?

*

11

Sam wants a spot of lunchtime reading, so she gets her plate of curd rice and beans curry ready and comes to my room to read my notes about Thatha.

I have had an uneventful morning. Some version of me had made a list of all the things I planned to accomplish during the time Appa and Amma were away at work. A hair mask and a long shower. Read about Tagore's poetry for my history essay. Clean the kitchen for Amma. Text all my (three) friends proactively.

Instead, I only managed a feeble text to my friend Alicia about therapy.

You know that therapist you went to last year, who was actually good, was she in Bangalore or Chennai? I can't remember.

I managed to shower, but not get dressed, so I lay in my old cloth towel, on my back, laptop half-open near me. I looked up at the ceiling and thought about sleeping and didn't sleep.

Sam shuffles around in my room, rearranging the things on Thatha's old dresser to set down her plate. It's rosewood and mahogany, domed mirror and drawers, stained with his coconut oil and Sam's Boroplus powder.

'It's really bad, okay? I'm warning you,' I say.

I open the file on my laptop and try to distract myself as she reads it.

She finishes in about three minutes. Sam has always been much faster at reading than I am. When the last Harry Potter book came out, Sam and Amma went to Landmark at 5 a.m. to buy it and brought home two copies. Sam and I raced to read it. I was only halfway through the book when Sam finished the whole thing and ran around the house.

'It's so depressing, Ami.' She puts down the laptop on my bed and looks at me as if we've both just left a movie theatre and are in bright light: she is blinking, readjusting, and my face is taking shape again.

'But it's all true.'

'So *what*! That just happened *once*.'

'Still, Sam.'

'Wait, I'll get myself a sweet.' Sam shuffles to the kitchen and I lie down on the bed.

I close my eyes and picture that day. Thatha shuffling in. His towel on my pillow, leaning against the upright pillow. Sam and I playing some ballroom song or the other on the Casio. Thatha sitting in silence, a half-smile on his face. Sam jumping on the bed, doing a two-step waltz.

'Sammy. Ami Barmy,' Thatha had said. 'How much I love you both, you know?'

Sam had continued to jump on the bed. 'Love you, Thatha! The mostest!'

I hadn't known what to say. Once Thatha had left the room, I hadn't known what to do either. The moment wouldn't leave my head. 'Sam, I should have said something! Right? What should I say?'

Sam walks back into the room and I sit up. She has brought in two bowls filled with pomegranate seeds; she gives me one. We munch contemplatively. She lies down next to me after we eat, lining up her shoulders with mine.

'Okay, Sammy, you tell me a nice story.' Sam's memories serve as an archive: down to the date, down to who was there and what they said, down to the microsecond. I love playing in her memories until she pulls me out, annoyed that it's up to her to remember everything for everyone.

'How about all the Krishna stories we used to talk about?' Sam asks.

'What stories?'

'Little Krishna stories. How he dragged himself on a barrel through the whole city to eat butter. And then one day, he tried to get fruit in exchange for rice, but when he ran over to the aunty to give her the rice, all the rice had fallen from his hands!'

'If Krishna was sooo great, how come . . .'

She is not impressed. She jabs her elbow into my stomach.

'Sam! Aaaah!'

'See, this is what I mean! Depressing! What about,' Sam continues, 'when I used to hide under Thatha's rocking chair when he watched TV, and I took some of his biscuits and his torch.'

Sam used to turn Thatha's rocking chair upside down to form a little wooden house and crawl inside it. She would then yell out the punchlines of the stories as Thatha told them.

And then Vasudeva bangs down the wall . . .

What wall?

The wall of his prison, *Ami!*

'I don't know why, Sam. I feel so bad about everything,' I say. I lean against her head and feel its familiar bumps against my head. Tears roll down my cheeks. Sam feels that I am crying but looks at the ceiling, not at me, for which she should win some kind of gallantry award.

I look up at the ceiling too.

'Can I ask you something?' Sam asks.

'Ask.' If I were Appa, I would have said, *Didn't you just ask me something?*

'You're not going back to college? I heard Appa in the morning. He said he'll break a deposit to pay your January fees.'

'Sammy.'

'Can I ask you something else?'

'Sam!'

'Can I?'

'Okay.'

'Do you have depression?'

'Maybe.' I push her arm with mine to indicate I want to topple the topic away.

Sam continues. 'It's just that a friend of mine, I can't tell you who, but a friend of mine has depression and for ages the doctor never realized what was happening. He said it's just teenagers' feelings, but then my friend asked the doctor,

"Do all teenagers want to kill themselves over this so-called 'feelings'?'"

'Oh my God,' I say.

On the ceiling, the glow-in-the-dark stars we once stuck up there still shine, though they have lost some of their glow. I remember that stars are already dead when we first see them. We are already too late.

Is that a good, poetic observation or is it trite?

'One more question. Last,' Sam says.

'Okay, ask.'

'Do you feel you have an emotional support system?'

'Since when do you know what that means?'

'Since the internet,' Sam says.

Sam knows everything. It's like she has lived through several rebirths and seen the kingdoms of Lumbini and Spartacus and Mars and has now returned, just to check in on everyone still slogging towards retirement in their first life.

'I read it's very important,' Sam says. 'So, do you?'

'I have you, don't I?' I poke Sam's hip and she links her arm with mine.

'But am I *supportive*? You can be honest,' Sam says solemnly. She tilts her head and her skull hits my clavicle.

'Aah! Sam! Of course you are. But sometimes I think I ask you to support me too much because you always let me ask you. Is that true? Now you better be honest. I need to know.'

'No. I'll tell you if you're annoying.'

Sam stays still, breathing slowly. She draws circles in the air as she talks, and it looks from this angle, like she has circled lines around the perimeter of the fan.

'What if I can never be normal again?' I ask. Saying it aloud sounds strangely shrill and tinny. Is that what I sound like?

I finally said it. To the world.

The fan turns, a line of dust on each blade.

'I say, forget about being normal,' Sam says. 'And forget about Appa. You took the time off to rest. So you should rest. It's like they say, you can't pour from an empty cup, Ami.'

'Yeah . . .' I burrow into my pillow. I press my eyes so close to the pillow fabric that the one-inch space looks endless, black, deep.

Sam insists upon a response. She sits up, on her knees. Her knee bangs into my arm and then my stomach as she sits up. She pokes me and looks down at me. 'You shouldn't keep thinking about January. That'll just make you tense all the time.'

Man. From this angle, she really seems like the bigger sister, not me.

'Don't tell anyone everything I just told you, otherwise I'll kill you.' I blink. 'Promise?'

'Promise.'

'God promise?'

'I'm not going to *God* promise, Ami. We're not five years old.'

I tickle her and she tickles me back until I lose the wrestling match. She sits on me, wrestler-style, for ten seconds. She wins, of course. She always does.

*

12

Writing draft/Notes about Thatha: 18 November 2013

When I was ten years old, we went to a wedding, or maybe it was an engagement, in a large hall with concrete rooms and airy ceilings. I was wearing a purple *pavadai* and an itchy purple blouse. I pulled at my blouse and wove through the groups of people sitting on chairs in front of the stage, under the fans.

'Amma,' I said, tugging at the skirt of her sari, but she was in a group of six, and they were all talking—bags and butterfly clips in laps, kerchiefs in hands and speaking in staccato, lyrical Tamil.

I was stopped by my tall cousin, who had: (1) gone to college and (2) a second ear piercing. She was talking to Thatha's scary sister, Roja. Roja had talc on her face—white on brown—and a jewel-purple sari that she pulled around herself, and a walking cane that she used not to walk, but to point at things she disapproved of. She asked me something very long and complicated, which I couldn't understand. I nodded. I smiled the same smile I had seen on everyone else's faces. This, however, did not work on Roja.

'*Enna, apdiye thalai aatariya*—are you just shaking your head or did you really understand?' Roja asked me. She then mimicked the way I nodded my head.

In a dejected way, I curled my toes and looked down at my feet, dressed as they were in my finest black Velcro sandals. I went and found Sam but it was no use—she was busy playing Flash with our cousins and had finally got cosy.

'I'm *playing*, Ami. Even you should join,' Sam said. 'Flash is more fun if more people play.'

Thatha passed by us on his way to the food station outside.

Sam jumped up on to the chair and drummed a beat on Thatha's bald head, and sang 'Money for Nothing' to the tune.

'That ain't working, that's the way you do it! You play the guitar on the MTV!' Sam whisper-yelled.

And then Thatha sang, '*Odi vilayadu paapa . . .*'

I ran and followed Thatha out of the room. I caught up with him at the door. 'Thatha,' I said, pulling his shirtsleeve. He was wearing a crisp pink one today. It reminded me of Gelusil, the sweet tablets Thatha always had lying around on his dresser. I used to run in and eat them until one day he found out they were only for stomach problems. 'I cannot give you any more,' he'd said sadly.

'But Thatha, my stomach is paining! Come on, just one!'

'Hello, Ami Barmy,' Thatha said, now. 'Come, let us go eat paan.'

'Thatha, I just want to go home, why can't Amma-Appa take me?'

'If you wish, I can come and drop you back home?' Thatha asked. 'We can go by auto.'

'No . . . It's okay,' I mumbled. 'I know you want to stay.'

Thatha waved at the paan counter, where people milled around. 'I have to stay, Ami Barmy, all my brothers and sisters are here and if I leave, I will miss out on everything.'

'I hate them,' I declared. 'They always speak so fast and I never understand them, and they're mean.'

'Why will you not understand? Try *panna takku-nu varo*,' Thatha explained. 'You got how much in your Tamil exam?'

'I got 48 on 50,' I said. 'That was cool.'

'Very cool, not just little cool.' Thatha smiled.

'But even if I become an expert, I will never talk to Roja, I promise,' I said.

The counter was covered in white cloth, lined with different plates to assemble paan: fans of green leaves, little pots of spicy pink paste, betel nuts and some sweet kernels.

'You want?' Thatha asked me.

'No . . . It's spicy.'

'Here, taste.' Thatha rolled up a green leaf and gave it to me. It was acidic and sharp and burnt the back of my throat.

Two of his cousins stood at the counter, just out of hearing distance. 'Ey, listen,' he called out at them. They walked over and I quickly hid behind him, close to the wall where paper covers were lined up as returned gifts, filled with bolts of silk, coconuts and packets of adhirsams. Sugar crystals were sprinkled all over the grey floor. The industrial whirring of the caterers in the dining hall was humming through the rooms.

'Ami has a fine piece of news . . .' Thatha looked down at me, his lips bright pink from the paan, and smiled. 'Tell them, no.'

'Nothing . . . I had a cycle test in Tamil and I got my marks and I got 48 on 50,' I mumbled.

'*Shabash*! Fantastic,' Thatha's cousin said and clasped my hand. He smelled like silk, starch and powder. I released his hand. They then started talking fast, and I frowned up at them.

In a gap in the conversation, Thatha looked down at me. 'I will take care of it, don't worry,' Thatha said. He then answered all their questions on my behalf and I ran away, filled with relief. I played with the loose sugar crystals and hid behind the table.

*

13

On Day Three of the writing class, I am no longer afraid of KGM. Like those people in *Rang De Basanti*, who walk to their deaths laughing. It's not that I feel more confident, exactly. I am just in that safe, painless spot when nothing can worry me any more because I have already worried about every tiny thing there is to worry about.

While I wait for the girls, I return *Tuesdays with Morrie* to the library. It was really not much help. It's a beautifully written, simple story, but it offers no real lessons on how to write about Thatha. Mitch remembers every interaction with Morrie, down to the potato salad and bagels in the fridge. I have a very poor memory and only remember fragments, floating in and out of my mind. I don't remember dates and seconds. I can't chart out a journey.

My next book is a Nicholas Sparks novel, *Nights in Rodanthe*. I read this during march-pasts too, after *The Notebook* and *A Walk to Remember*, thinking I'd found some offbeat Sparks gem only I knew about.

Let's see if this one helps.

By the time all the girls trickle in, it is half an hour into the class and I am still downstairs, reading and working on the class worksheets. I see Michael, walking in criss-cross steps, giving the library teacher his register to sign something.

'Hi, Michael.'

He points at my books. 'All ready?'

'Ready.'

'Go and get full marks.'

'I'm teaching Sam and her friends, so they should get full marks, not me,' I say. I smile at him and he clicks his tongue and shoos me upstairs.

Sam, Deeksha and Lavanya are buzzing around at our usual table. I sit by the window, next to Sam. I feel calm, methodical, like I'm making a cup of coffee. Deeksha has the poetry textbook open to 'Ode on a Grecian Urn'. I pass around three large pieces of paper I've torn out from my spiral notebook. On each of them, I've drawn out two columns, one to write about objects and one for writing about whatever feelings those objects inspire.

'Akshita isn't here today either,' Deeksha says. The three girls look at each other, like they're all in on a secret.

I want to tell them I don't mind if they leave me out of secrets; I understand that everyone has a big and ephemeral world they can't share with anyone else, just like I can't share what I'm thinking with them. I consider whether I should say this.

Am I being pretentious again?

Deeksha speaks. 'Anyway . . . Object poems?'

She and Lavanya are swivelling in their chairs, which creak at the movement. 'I'll start,' Deeksha says. She opens her blue velvet notebook. She reads:

'Nothing special, just five inches by two
The badge is chrome and silver,
Its brass gleam is bright in the rays
of the sun; it doesn't move, doesn't erase
Its pin pricked my finger when I put it on
And stared at the sea of friends, seniors, juniors
I felt free
I felt like everyone was there just to celebrate me
I never wanted to feel special or chosen or rare
But for a few moments I swear I was walking on air.'

'I know,' she says. 'It doesn't fully rhyme, but—'

'That's okay,' I cut her off. 'Everything doesn't have to rhyme. It doesn't matter. That was damn good.' I nod. I can feel how much effort Deeksha put into the poem. 'You were talking about a real badge?'

She pulls it out of her skirt pocket—it is silver and rectangular, and it says 'Deeksha Rao, Student Council.' The edge of Deeksha's badge is cracked. It's large in her hand, almost comically so. She places it on the table and it glints a brilliant white when catching the light.

'It's the dumbest thing in the world. Sharon randomly picks whoever she likes and it's always the most annoying people,' Lavanya says. 'Then they pretend it's such an honour. Plus, their taste in prefects is horrible. Except for you, Deeksha. Remember Shilpa, who was captain last year? She's giving us a Careers speech this year, of all people.'

'Shilpa was sort of useless,' Deeksha agrees.

I steer the conversation back to the subject. 'Okay, Deeksha, maybe you could add some connection in the poem that bridges the object to something else, too—you know how you talked about feeling like nobody hears you? I like the description of how you felt, maybe add more things like that.'

'Okay. I'll do that,' Deeksha says, drawing a tiny zigzag on her paper. 'I've wanted to be a prefect all my life, at least most of my school life, and I thought I had to do so much to get it, make sure everyone knew me. Like everyone should want to save me from a well. For some reason, that's how I measured it. How many people would notice if you fell in a well and would come and save you? But it's weird, now that I'm finally a prefect, there's all this extra attention and pressure on me. It doesn't feel exactly like I thought it would.'

The badge glints in the light. The etching reveals silver below, where the black ink is fading.

Deeksha scribbles on her piece of paper.

'Okay, Sam, your turn,' Lavanya says, bolt-cutting through the silence.

'Uhh . . . Okay, fine. So, I'm going to read what I wrote about my favourite object,' Sam clarifies. She opens her poetry textbook to the very last page, where her large circular writing swoops in arcs along the page between the printed words, in between margins.

'When I was really young, maybe eight years old, I would sometimes go for walks with my grandfather, and we'd stop at a different place each time, on the same grey road, like it popped up just for us. Whenever we stopped at a stationery shop, he would get me a single pen, and one for himself too. He'd hook it into his shirt pocket and then throw out the old pen. I still have the pen he gave me, which still works—maybe it runs on unlimited cartridges or maybe it's just a new pen and I didn't notice, because every plastic retractable ballpoint pen feels like that pen to me. In the hierarchy of pens, it's nowhere near Pilot V5 or even a leaky Parker pen. But it has one advantage:

it's immortal and has weathered every element in the world. Therefore, it is mightier than swords.'

I smile, remembering Thatha's slow, shuffling footsteps and Sam's clattering, raindrop-like running in harmony. Thatha looking down at a tiny, bobbing Sam. Sam holding Thatha's hand to make sure he didn't slip as he walked. Thatha walking into the room as we played the Casio. *Sammy and Ami Barmy.* The ups, downs of the hums of the fan, my silence.

'Technically, would you call that a poem, is my question,' Deeksha says. 'Can we classify that as a poem, Ami?'

'It could be a prose poem,' I said. 'Like what we're going to do later . . .'

Lavanya's words overlap with mine. 'Yeah, or you can always change it later . . . Oh wait, Sam, that's your granddad, right? The same one I met.'

'I think I met him too, right?' Deeksha says.

'No, you met my dad,' Sam says. 'Only Akshita and Lavanya have met my granddad.'

'But didn't he come, for Report Card day, you guys met me and my mom . . .' Deeksha's words overlap with Sam's.

'No,' Sam said. 'You've never met him, I'm telling you, that was my dad.'

'Do you have the pen?' Deeksha asks.

'Obviously,' Sam says. Like a magician or a film star, she pulls the pen, on cue, out of her backpack: a royal-blue cartridge in a thin, cylindrical plastic case; and a cracked cap, thin, thinner than a finger. A smile glimmers on her face, like light reflected in a swimming pool.

'Oh my God. It's so . . . tiny,' Lavanya says. She rolls it down the table, and each of its perfectly flat sides stops as the pen rolls. 'I think I pictured the Avenger of pens.'

'Okay, so you should focus on the actual memory, not just the pen,' Deeksha says.

'Yeah, Sam, either you could focus on that day or you can change around the form and line length,' I say.

It's Sam's turn to scribble now, leaning close to the table, almost parallel with it.

'Ami, your turn,' Deeksha looks up.

I stare at them. It's somehow easy to talk. 'I've also been thinking about my granddad and that yellow Casio keyboard I was telling you about. He sometimes used to come into our room and listen to us play it. It feels like all that is just gone. Even the Casio's plug doesn't work any more.'

The Casio is now on a high shelf of my cupboard. None of the buttons respond when I poke at them. The minor keys have turned grey and there is no waltz floating out of its tiny speakers.

'Same theme as Sam,' Lavanya says, her head still bobbing, as she contemplates me. Her face is translucent, as usual. She is deliberate about everything, every tilt of the head and every flicker of the eye.

'So what did you write, Ami?' Deeksha says.

I lean back on my chair and feel that slight vertigo when the chair almost falls over, but then doesn't. Shadows of the window grilles fall on the wall opposite me, behind Sam and Deeksha, dancing above their heads. From downstairs, the sounds of groups of two and three people chatting behind their textbooks float up, low like buzzing bees.

'I think . . . I think I'm stuck. I've been trying to write about this for a month actually.'

'But you're amazing at writing,' Lavanya says.

'She just gets in her own head,' Sam says. 'She's a chronic overthinker.'

Deeksha nods, pursing her lips. She taps her pen on the desk. 'You do seem that way,' she tells me.

We laugh at this diagnosis. Sam leans over and pats my hand. 'Don't worry,' she says. 'We'll fix you.'

'By the end of these classes you'll be able to write a whole epic, not just a one-pager,' Deeksha says.

'So how long has this problem been going on?' Lavanya asks me.

The three girls peer at me, like lab technicians, waiting for me to list out my symptoms.

I think about the time I sat here in this library, six years ago, after my history exam and before my geography exam. I had typed out a letter on the computer:

Dear Thatha,
My geography exam is tomorrow! I don't know if I'll remember anything! But if I study more, won't I forget everything?

Would he even see this—was there even a point? It had been twenty-one days since he died.

Slow dissolve: back to present.

'A long time,' I say.

There's a low thump in the library and Siddharth walks in, spectacles on, uniform shirt a bit loose for him, slight stubble.

'Have you guys seen Akshita?' he asks.

'No,' Deeksha says. 'You also haven't?'

He shrugs and runs back down the steps, two at a time.

Sam looks at me and says, 'Oh, Akshita and Siddharth broke up again yesterday.' I give Sam a secret-signal look, silently asking: *Did Siddharth coming over the other day have anything to do with this?* But she looks away. I cannot ask Sam anything more in such a public setting, so I return to my role.

'Okay, so your object, Lavanya.'

'Mine is a little bit difficult to explain—' she starts.

Before Lavanya can talk any more about her object, she gets distracted by something she sees through the library window, on the parking lot: 'Oh my God, look!'

I peer out, and Sam and Deeksha prop themselves up on their elbows to look out of the window. We see Akshita and Siddharth standing on the field, next to a parked car, and they are talking—firm stances, standing six feet apart from each other, like they barely know the person in front of them. This goes on for a few minutes. Then they speak and stare and the girls peer down from the window.

'My God. That doesn't look good,' Deeksha says. 'Should we do something?'

Sam shakes her head. 'I still haven't heard about Lavanya's object—'

'Sam . . . she's—' Deeksha says.

'Guys, we shouldn't get involved,' Sam says, overlapping with Deeksha.

'No, wait, I'll just go check,' Deeksha says. 'You guys continue. One sec.' Deeksha does a two-step shuffle and runs out of the library, out of sight.

Lavanya swivels back to me and moves to sit opposite Sam and me, now that it's just the three of us.

'So it's just us,' I say. 'Shall we wrap up?'

'No, no, I can continue, I don't mind.' Lavanya smiles at me. 'Oh, it's my turn. I can show you guys the object I wrote about. It's up in the art room.'

'Oh, sure.'

Sam is looking out through the window. She slumps, takes in a deep breath. 'Can I just go get a brownie?' Sam asks. 'I'm hungry.'

'Want me to come?' Lavanya asks.

'No, no.' Sam stands up, checks her pocket, makes sure there are some folded rupee notes in it. 'I need to not be around anyone for a while.'

* * *

Sam walks across the parking lot, and Lavanya and I go upstairs to the art room: it's three floors up, at the very top of the building. It's secluded enough to always have cool grey light instead of hot white light, and there are rows of low tables, a sink to mix paint and canvases piled high on top of wardrobes. There are always plastic plates with half-dried paint, congealed brushes and cotton cloths daubed with paint lining every table in the room.

Lavanya opens the cupboard, while I sit in a corner. She pulls out papers from the 'Class 11' shelf, until she finds a large piece of sketch paper. She gives it to me. It's a bouquet of roses, arranged in a green vase: a still life. On the stem of each rose and along the base of the vase, are written words. Maybe lyrics or thoughts or just a signature. I don't look too closely: there are some things I don't need to know. Each red or pink or blue rose is a different shade, lightened with water differently. Little smudges of grey surround the roses. Some petals are fading; some fallen leaves linger in the muddy water of the vase. In the background of the still life is a switchboard, and a wire: little details.

'Lavanya, this is beautiful! You're so talented.'

She shakes her head, batting the compliment back like we're engaged in a tennis rally. Reflexively, she shakes the paper to dry the already-dry paint.

'Drawing is a little easier. Writing is tougher,' she says.

'Maybe the writing class will help you, just to be with everyone,' I say. 'Like you know, Tagore won the Nobel Prize because Ezra Pound found his writing and read it out to a group of writers in London.'

Lavanya waggles her eyebrows and smoothens out her art again. 'See, I get it, but it's just difficult,' Lavanya says.

'Okay, here.' I grab a Nataraj Bold pencil and a piece of abandoned newspaper from near the sink. I draw six blanks for six words.

'Look at this six-word story by Hemingway. "For sale: baby shoes, never worn."'

I write the story down.

'That's it? The full story?'

'The full story.' I do an orchestrator's flourish with my hands.

'Okay, I can write that much.'

'Good.'

We lean back on the counter and look out at the field. It's nearly 4 p.m. and the air is turning golden.

'Listen, that was a nice class today, Ami. Sorry about . . . all the confusion,' Lavanya says.

'Don't be silly! No need to worry about that.'

'I was really scared Akshita would actually come to the class today and say something. So it's good only she didn't come.'

'Scared? Why?'

'I don't know . . .' she mumbles. 'Did Sam not tell you? At Deeksha's party, Akshita was upset with Sam, and she said she was so angry, and she even said she wants to, you know . . .' Lavanya points at her wrist with her other hand, moving it away slowly.

'Because of all this. She spent some one hour locked in the bathroom and we tried to get her to come out.'

'What? What happened?'

The light ripples against Lavanya's face as she turns away from the window. 'Sam didn't tell you?'

I cover up. 'No, she did. I just don't remember. I don't know Akshita and Siddharth too well, so I get confused . . .'

Lavanya nods and shakes out the paper with the Hemingway story.

I look out through the window.

Sam's shadow is visible on the field, while she stands and counts her change, before she disappears into the golden distance.

*

14

Sam and I used to love early mornings. We would wake up when everything in the house was still silent, still a pale liquid grey-blue. When the sun slowly rose and turned everything a warm yellow, we used to feel like we had won some race.

I wake Sam up. She's sleeping with her back to the door, with ten pillows all around her, like a fortress. Her arms and back are soft when I jump on to the bed.

'Saaaaam.'

There are two gulmohar trees visible from her window, moving softly, their red flowers flowing on a green sea. Below us, the tyre swing on the tree creaks slowly and the Adyar River curls, deep green, towards the bridge.

'What do you want?' she says into her pillow. The patchwork quilt has left marks on her arm.

'Wake up, no.'

'Why?'

'Just for fun.'

We walk into the kitchen in a single file—I tiptoe and she shuffles, her feet hissing against the ground, a consistent slow beat. She sits on the countertop, frowning in the pale light. Her hair is curling to one side—the side she sleeps on. It falls in curtains to her shoulders.

I put the pan on the stove, fill it with water and tea, watch it bubble. 'So,' I say, putting the steel canister of tea leaves back in the cupboard. 'Lavanya told me about this Akshita and the Birthday-and-Bathroom situation.'

'I don't want to talk about it,' she says. But she looks slightly to the left when she speaks, and her face cracks like a walnut. So I know she really does want to talk about it.

'Okay, we won't talk about it,' I say.

I can feel her watching me as I add milk, ginger, cardamom pods. When the tea boils, I pour it into two old mugs—one says 'PARIS' and the other says 'NUMBER ONE DAD'—and hand her one.

'Terrace?' I ask her.

We climb up to the terrace in the complex. The bricks are still cool under our feet. Soon they will turn too hot to walk on. We will have to run, somehow using only our big toes. We sit on the brick-red ground, the two mugs betwen us.

'So . . .' I start again.

'I know you want to talk, Ami, but nothing is up,' Sam says, frowning at me, the steam from her tea fogging up her glasses. Crows whine, parrots chirp, ants crawl on our thighs and Sam's glasses clear up.

'Okay, forget it, tell me something else. What fan fiction are you reading?' I ask.

'That's private.'

'Didn't you win some reader award? What a star.'

'I'm not a *star*. It's not a big deal to win. I just got Top Reader Points.'

'What does that give you?'

'Nothing. You get to comment on your favourite writers' stuff before it releases and there's this one writer . . .' Sam stops and drinks her tea. 'I see what you're doing. Don't try and trick me into talking.'

'Who's tricking anyone?'

'I know you want to ask me about Akshita, and I'm not responsible for anyone, okay? Not responsible for Akshita's life.'

I blink at her. She's deliberately looking away, off at a tree in the distance. The light makes her eyes look pale hazel. I don't know what she means, but I know better than to ask.

'I know, Sam.'

'So as soon as I reached the party with Siddharth, Akshita started yelling at me. I think they were back together that day. As if anyone can keep track. She said I shouldn't have come with him. And I'm not even interested in him. Isn't it heteronormative to assume I am? He's just my friend and you have to make an effort with friends, right? He messaged me first about Deeksha's party, you know. Usually, I have to message people first and I hate that. So I was happy, and I wanted to do as I would like done to me.'

'And then what happened?'

'*Nothing*, Ami, why is it so important?' Sam slurps her tea, and it ripples on the surface.

'It's not important,' I say. I stare down at my feet and pluck at the dry skin near my toes so that she won't feel self-conscious.

'We had been standing near the bathroom door for an hour while she was inside.' Sam looks down at her mug and crosses her legs. 'She never opened the door. I kept knocking. Someone said they heard her say "Sam". And everyone thought it was my fault she was there. Actually, I thought that too.'

'Then what happened?'

'She finally came out and then Deeksha distracted everyone so that we could go back to the beach. And Siddharth and I didn't talk the rest of the time. I just talked to Deeksha and Lavanya and then right after the cake, Lavanya dropped me home in her car.'

'So you just stood there awkwardly?'

'Yeah.' The first car sounds start, on the street below. From the police training academy down the road, the trainees, all in navy blue, jog past in twos and threes.

'Do you think I'm doing something wrong?' Sam asks.

When I turn around and look back at her, it's like I'm returning from a great distance to the moment in front of me. 'No,' I say. 'I think you're smart.'

'Why?'

'Some people are just like that.'

'No, I mean *why*.'

'Because you're right, you can't do anything about Akshita and Siddharth's relationship. And it's not like you're doing anything to interfere, right, even if Akshita thinks so.'

'She told me she feels bad that I'm prettier than her. So I told *her*, for the millionth time, all about the latest project I'm on, to stop caring about how I look,' Sam says. 'Like in *The Perks of Being a Wallflower*.'

'What happens in that?'

'Mary Elizabeth says she doesn't want to be complimented about how she looks because she can't control her appearance or do anything about it,' Sam says, talking fast. 'I told Akshita she should be happy the way she is. And I don't care about Siddharth. Didn't you read it? I told you so many times.' Sam sits on her knees and leans forward.

'I did, in September, I think. I don't remember that part.'

I frown, thinking about Sam standing outside a locked door at Deeksha's party, the sound of the beach softly whooshing outside, maybe people eating orange stick ice creams as the sun slowly set, the night turned purple and the sand turned golden. The breeze heavy and salty right before the night unrolled itself. Sam's hands folded across her body, in that grey top, wondering if it was her fault and wondering what the 'it' was and wondering who would come and save her.

I think of Akshita, too, on the other side of the door, fully aware she was being irrational but sure that she had to do something about Siddharth, anything, because if she didn't then everything else would tumble and change too, knowing she didn't need to worry about Sam but worrying anyway, on the off-chance that she needed to. Looking around the bathroom to find the sharpest object, even though she wouldn't actually do anything—just wanting the option. Just wondering if she should.

Sam slurps her tea some more.

'Can you believe Akshita and I used to be best friends?' she asks.

'I know.'

'Now I have to figure out everything all over again.' Sam lets these words rest in the air before she decides it's time to get up and go downstairs. I love and rue how she can swing between thoughtfulness and action, in under two minutes. Things take me a little bit longer.

The sunlight is no longer grey: it slowly turns golden. The dogs start barking, on the street below, a volley, one sound blending into another.

In college, when I would be sitting in my room, I would always call up Sam, to see her scrambly, pixelated face, and ask her to talk to me about nothing in particular, just to hear the comforting sound of her voice, and whatever she had done that day. She always took my call.

One day, I called Sam because I couldn't sleep. I asked her to tell me a nice story. We talked about an episode of *Parks and Recreation* for half an hour, and then Sam's voice flagged, got slower.

'Okay, Ami, my phone has to charge.'

'So you can charge it and talk.'

She waited. The line crackled. In the background, her freshly painted lilac walls (our room used to be yellow and green) reflected the light from her lampshade.

'It's not just that,' she said. 'I'm tired. I want to hang up.'

*

15

I walk back downstairs when the heat gets too strong. Sam is curled up like a bean, reading in the hall, and Amma and Appa are sitting in the dining room. Amma is drinking freshly squeezed orange juice and Appa has a bowl filled with an array of tablets set before him.

'Listen to this,' Appa says, pushing the newspaper towards Amma.

'The government is getting more and more autocratic,' Amma says.

'You can't say that,' Appa says. 'You can't just say that. You have to come up with a solution.'

'Hello, why should I? They get almost half our salary every year. They should.'

'Hey,' I say.

'Coffee?' Amma asks.

'No, thanks.' I sit down next to them. 'So listen. We have to do something about Sam.'

Amma takes a sip of juice. 'What happened to her?'

'Nothing, I've been seeing in all the writing classes that she and Akshita have this weird tension and I think it's stressing her out. She's under a lot of pressure, she says she barely talks to her any more and she has to avoid her, and it must be weighing on her.'

Appa simultaneously flips a page of the newspaper and pulls his phone closer to him.

'Appa.'

'Hm?' He looks up. 'What, Ami, nothing happened to Sam.'

'I'm telling you, she feels stressed out and trapped.'

'Trapped?' Amma asks. 'She told you this?'

'Not literally, but I sensed it.'

'I'll talk to her,' Amma says.

'No, Ma, don't, I don't want her to feel self-conscious. I'm just saying. This whole thing with Akshita, she just feels . . .'

'We met Hiral, Shekar. Akshita's mother. At Gangotree. Remember?' Amma asks Appa.

'They're divorced, right? Her parents?' I ask.

'Separated, but listen, she has no problem asking for a loan for him,' Appa says. 'He called me just the other day. Hema, I told you? First, she messaged, then this bugger called. Kept calling until I picked up. Wanted some business loan extension. As if I'm one loan agent.'

'So what did you say?' I ask.

'I told him I'll try my best, what else will I say. He seemed happy only, he was telling me they're doing some store extension, special line with sapphires or something. Akshita is also involved in planning it. See. Nothing's wrong, Ami. Just because you were sad in school, doesn't mean everyone is sad.'

Amma tilts her head and reaches her arm out to me.

'You worry too much, Ami,' Amma says.

'Can you please listen to me?'

'Ami,' Appa says. 'You don't need to create a problem where no problem exists.'

'I'm telling you, it exists! What's your plan? What are you going to do about it?'

'Sam isn't like you. If she has a problem, she'll tell us,' Appa said. 'Okay?'

It's sticky. I'm hot and tired and frustrated. I wonder how long I have before I yell and/or cry.

I try to think about what Sam would do.

Just go, stupid, don't wait until it becomes a fight.

'I'm going to shower,' I say.

'Make sure the geyser is on,' Amma says, taking another sip of her juice. The fan creaks on the ceiling.

'Every day there is less and less hot water in the geyser,' Appa says.

'You have to switch it on in time, only then hot water will be there,' Amma says.

I leave the room and they don't notice they've left yet another conversation incomplete.

*

16

On Day Four of the writing class, I linger on the bench behind the canteen, hoping that if I go in fifteen minutes late, everyone else will be in class. I lean back on the bench, trying my best to forget about my appointment with Nirmal later in the day.

There's no one here, just the back of the canteen, the half-open entrance, the white wall of the compound, the trellised shade from the trees. I open my book and try to read, but I stay on the same page, my eyes hazy and forming flowery shapes on the page. *Nights in Rodanthe* is too perfect. More people with perfect memory. Adrienne knows exactly what she and Paul talked about during that one week, twenty years ago.

When Michael walks past, I am momentarily distracted and snap a photograph of him.

I title it *Michael, Principal's Assistant*. Michael sees.

'Give my full title,' Michael says, holding his register up like a shield or an umbrella. His blue shirt is too loose for him, hanging almost to the knee of his navy-blue trousers. His slippers—black leather, grey sole, worn—are clacketing as always.

'Senior Peon/Principal Assistant,' Michael says.

'Plus now the canteen manager,' I say.

'Ah, you write that also.'

I walk up the library stairs and see the girls' faces, tiny, floating like candles on a lake. I smile even though I feel heavy, leaden weights inside my body, and my neck feels like it will snap. I wipe down all my feelings and force a cheer into my voice.

'Hey guys,' I say. 'Are you ready?' I put down the papers and slide them to each of the girls. I sit by the window, Akshita next to me, Sam and Lavanya opposite me. Deeksha is at the head of the table. The air through the window is cool, but my hands shake a little bit as I pass the sheets of paper. I look down at them. This has never happened before.

'So today . . . Actually, Akshita,' I turn to her. 'Let me tell you what you missed last time first. We're doing object poems, but the six-word story version. So it's an object story.'

I wonder if my talking despite my symptoms makes me seem like a cool, suffering protagonist on a procedural, like *House M.D.* At the same time, I am aware of an ache in my hand.

'I know, Deeksha told me, sorry I missed last time, I had this other class . . .' Akshita runs out of steam mid-sentence.

I move my hand away, fast, before Sam realizes it now has a life of its own and is shaking like a trapped fish.

Deeksha is too tall for her chair. She creaks, swivelling, and bends her arms around the chair.

'Okay, so, the badge—' Deeksha starts off before another voice chimes in.

'Oh my God, Ami! You realize something? You've finished half the classes! I just realized. Congrats!' It's Lavanya.

'Hey, that's true.' Sam smiles. The school bell rings and voices echo and tumble down the stairs outside the library. 'School ends on 15 December. Wait, so only three classes are left. More than half over.'

'Oh my God, we have so much left to do,' Deeksha now frowns, leaning forward. 'So, Ami, Sam and I had an idea. Should we add a section with our poetry in the *Digest*? Like it can be the first Lit Soc thing.'

'We can add them on the last three pages, you know, right after the class photos,' Sam says.

'Don't worry about the formatting and all that, I'll do it.' Deeksha nods at her.

'Sure,' I tell them. 'You should put all your writing in, for sure. How much you've done in such a short time.'

'And we're not even writers, imagine. I think we did decently considering that.' Deeksha looks around at everyone for their votes of confidence.

'Not just decent, look at this, you're expressing yourself, and it's so emotionally honest. That's the whole point of this class, not to become the next . . .' I fish around for the right word. 'Murakami.' There. I just decided the point of this class, like a *Dead Poets Society* with lower emotional stakes— and more meandering conversation. I, of course, am yet to make my breakthrough. I think of the few lines in my own essay: thin, wandering centipedes petering out into nothing. The thought of my name next to the class photos fills me with something that can best be described as blankness.

'So, Deeksha, the badge,' I say, commencing the class with a fresh sense of direction. 'Let's start there now?' I look at her.

We discuss the six-word stories we can create using Deeksha's badge, Lavanya's painting and Akshita's mother's emerald ring. We turn to Sam, who taps on her sheet of paper. I can see her spirally, swoopy handwriting, as looping into Ss and Os. 'God, this is suddenly so difficult,' she says. '"Thatha's Gone, but His Pen Still Writes".'

'Maybe "works" is better,' Lavanya says. '"Pen still writes" is like it's some ghost pen. "Thatha is Gone, but His Pen Still Works".'

'Okay, Ami, your turn,' Sam raises her eyebrows at me, her outside-voice nice and low and grainy.

'Yes. I'll talk about my Casio.'

'What's the feeling?' Deeksha asks.

'Nostalgia, probably,' Sam answers.

'At least give me a chance.' I stare at them.

The words spill out of me:

I can't remember anything. Every time I try, all my memories run out of my mind, like cats running out of a house. It was a warm evening, and I was eleven years old. Maybe I was twelve. It doesn't matter. You always said your birthdays didn't matter. Pick any date!

Sam and I were playing, when we pressed pause on the song. The music was so stereo-sound, so high-key. You sat down, and the room paused when the song paused.

Tell me, if you can, how I can go back there, and say:

Stay a little longer.

Do you want to press buttons on the keyboard, see what happens? This key is cymbals, this key is harpsichord. If you press the button at the top, a song plays. I think it's a river waltz or maybe a polka dance.

Do you want to know anything about me? Do you want to ask me anything?

Carry on, you said.

No, no, not yet.

I look up. I feel like Tagore at that reading, in some underground living room in Bloomsbury or Euston, the air black with rain and the inside cosy with firelight, reading *Gitanjali*: every word so simple, a quick axe-cut, leaving a straight line.

Deeksha, Sam and Lavanya, however, do not look like that cosy group.

Deeksha is the first to speak. 'How the hell should we fit this into six words?!'

*

17

The afternoon light is a mellow kind of yellow. I take a cab to Nirmal's, past the usual sights of the Aavin Milk Depot, the convention centre with stiff cotton saris, and the stalls selling bamboo blinds. I put on my earphones, but it is truly impossible to choose a song.

What is the perfect song for finding out your test results that will probably prove that everything isn't normal? You aren't normal? Not an old song, not a new song, no Tamil and no Hindi. No indie and no cheesy pop. Nothing too sad, in case I am too buzzy and distracted to even handle Nirmal. Nothing too loud. I just listen to the hums of traffic, see endless people pause and resume, on two-wheelers, mid-conversation, at traffic signals.

The cab brings me up, like a limo, to Nirmal's before I choose a song. It's on the ground floor of a small bungalow; a wrought-iron grilled balcony hides a porch. A sign saying 'Beware of Dog'. Little night-jasmine petals by the gate. People's chappals in a pile on the ground.

The receptionist, guarding a ten-chair, badly lit waiting room, is happy. 'No queue today. Go, go.'

'Thanks . . .' I pause, but she doesn't tell me her name.

There's no queue, but I still have to wait outside for Nirmal to get off the phone. I look at the view: a locked brown door, and strangely, a carrom board stacked on its side in the corner. Some depressing art: hyper pixelated, impossibly saturated digital prints of water falling on to rocks; three puppies with melting chocolate eyes wearing bunny ears.

I send Sam a picture. *What do you think this means?*

Then I message Amma. *Just reached.*

Amma replies: *Cool, keep me posted,* followed by five fingers-crossed signs.

Sam replies: *Yuck!!!! I wish they had Monet's water lilies.*

I resolve to pass on the message to Nirmal.

Nirmal's office is a ten-by-ten-foot room filled with things: an old desktop computer; a desk; a patient's table; a large Ajanta wall clock; a sepia photograph of a man; certificates for expertise in neuropsychiatry and personality disorders; a steel stool; a CCTV camera of the waiting room.

'Ah, Ami, dear,' Nirmal says, standing up when she sees me.

Kishore Kumar is playing on the radio. I look around and can't see where the song is coming from, as if the tinny, beautiful voice fills the air itself. *Am I in the afterlife?*

'Hi . . .' I say, and pause. Do I call her Nirmal or Doctor? 'I like the song,' I say instead.

She doesn't say anything. reaches out her hand to shake mine. Her hand is dry and papery. 'Please sit, dear. You have grown up so much. Now here is where I show my age and say you were this tall or this short . . . Sit, dear, please.'

I sit. Nirmal gestures at her file, or rather, my file. A thick sheaf of papers sits inside a folder marked with the hospital's logo: heart in hands, a mint green sea wave.

'So tell me, Ami. How are you doing?'

'Good, a bit stressed about this appointment, but good.'

'Don't be stressed. Take a breath in.'

'Sorry?'

'Breathe, dear. We get so caught up in moving around, this, that, we forget that half our problems will be solved if we just take in a breath. You will be surprised at how many patients I tell to do the same.'

She taps her pen against her prescription pad, stares at me with an unwavering, watchful look, leans forward with her arm balancing on her desk. There are wrinkles near her temples, and she smells like fabric starch. I now have a vague memory of her, outside Thatha's room, putting her phone inside the front pocket of her Hidesign bag, her short hair silhouetted against the open front door.

I breathe. One in, five out. I breathe perfectly, to bypass her telling me how to do it. She is satisfied.

'All right, Ami, dear, how are we feeling today?'

'Good.'

'All right. Shall we proceed?'

'Sure.'

'So your mother tells me you came back from the UK earlier, before the term finished. And you have done all your tests. So tell me. What do you think is the issue?'

O what can ail thee, knight-at-arms?

'I came back because I just needed some time,' I say, very well rehearsed in my head. 'I went to a college counsellor there once, before I came back. I don't know, it felt like I was just stressed . . . or something . . . all the time. I couldn't really focus on work, people, anything . . .' I take a pause. 'I feel . . . I think . . . I just feel like something was wrong with me, but I didn't know what it was . . .'

'I see. And since returning?' Nirmal's phone rings. She turns it on silent and flips it on its side. There is a hundred-rupee note crammed into the pocket of the phone case.

Returning, I say to myself in my head. I think of seagulls. Or is it cranes? Suddenly, I can hear every single second of the ticking clock. I hear a game someone in the waiting room is playing, little flourishes after collecting digital diamonds. I hear a motorcycle horn. Kishore Kumar still sings.

'I did the tests and everything . . . I guess I just want to know . . . if something is wrong. Do I have a disorder?'

Will me wanting something to be wrong with me somehow bias Nirmal? Will she think something is even more wrong with me? What am I even thinking?

Nirmal smiles.

'Tell me your symptoms. Whatever is striking you if you think.'

'I'm just tired, I can't focus, I worry a lot, my thought patterns are a bit . . . And I feel tired.'

'Every day? Most days?'

'For some time every day.'

'Are you sleeping as you regularly do? More? Less?'

Like adding salt to kovakkai curry. *Little more?*

'The usual, I think. I sleep around eleven . . .' I think back to that moment before sleep, which sometimes passes fast and sometimes stays like a rain cloud. 'I wake up at seven.' Because Amma is talking, clattering, opening doors around then. Sunlight slowly fills the house, waking up slowly, after Amma. In college, I used to wake up only when the garbage trucks wheeled the ten-foot-high bins down the back lanes outside my window, a loud rumbling, the views broken into grids by scaffolding.

'Right,' Nirmal says. She taps at the file. 'It is quite clear here. You have mild strains of clinical depression and very much of anxiety.'

Thank God.

Or . . . maybe not?

I don't know.

I focus on the small details: the blue vein on her right hand, the cream stripe on her blue polo-neck shirt, the Tupperware box under her desk, filled with sweet lime rinds.

'All right.'

'Would you like to discuss this?'

No.

'Sure.'

Nirmal explains depression and anxiety both—the lows and the jitters—but I don't remember what she says exactly. I just nod at the words that filter through to me: irritable and intelligence and energy and perception.

'But most importantly, dear, you can easily manage them and live a healthy and productive life. I can definitely help you. Are you overwhelmed?' She taps her pen against her prescription pad; it lands softly. 'Usually, people sit here for hours. One patient sat for so long, asking so many questions . . .' She looks more closely at me.

'No, I went to my college counsellor, and you know, they had these little books . . . How to identify . . . and then all kinds of illnesses. You know? So maybe . . .' I look down at my palms.

'I spent some time there, you know,' Nirmal says. 'In the UK. Mostly in Cambridge. It was so easy to drive there.

Here, just one main road makes me deaf . . . Tell me how you feel, dear. Take your time.'

I look up at her and she is just looking right at me.

'I know other people suffer . . . But I just didn't think I was sad enough . . . if that's what I'm supposed to think? Or anxious enough.'

We both, or maybe I just imagine this, look to the side: the closed door, the version of myself that no longer exists.

I look at the lizard under the tube light on the wall.

'Is that like a specific subspecies?' I ask. 'Of lizard. The domesticated tube light lizard.'

Nirmal gracefully accepts my need to change the topic. She turns around and looks at the lizard. The light falls slant on her hair.

She isn't talking, which makes me nervous. I feel I need to say something to indicate my emotional thought process. Something revealing about who I am as a person. I think of Amma, appearing from the kitchen doorway, giving Nirmal tea in a ceramic mug. What did the mug say? I can picture it, if I really think . . . It's still there now, hung up above the sink in a line with all the other mugs, their faces tilted towards the sun . . . Did it say 'DON'T TALK TO ME BEFORE COFFEE' in a cheery bubble font?

'My mother says I do this a lot,' I say.

'What?'

'Ask unanswerable questions.'

'Aha?' She is waiting for more.

Or maybe the mug had little volume levels: mood after one coffee. Two. Three.

'Your mother is a lovely lady,' Nirmal says, laying her hand flat on the desk. 'So strong. I was speaking to her after a long time when she called to tell me about you. What do you ask her, do you remember any questions?'

'I don't know. I'll let you know if I remember.'

'Please do,' Nirmal says. 'Please do, dear. You should keep a note. Sometimes we forget things . . .' She waves her hand around her temples, like she's catching air.

'If we do not keep a note. And now that you are my patient, I would like to know. Will you tell me?' She looks down at her notes. 'How do you feel about medication?'

'Sure,' I say. Then I realize that didn't really answer her question directly. I feel great about medication but don't want to seem insane. She starts writing, a scribble, every wave a crest, a cliché of a doctor's penmanship.

'Very small dosage for you, to start with. Let us see how you find it. If it is useful, you will see a visible improvement.'

She passes me the prescription pad.

'You can buy these medicines from the receptionist right outside the office. And you make another appointment, you come back in one week.'

'Sure.'

'If anything is required, call. I find it difficult to respond on message,' Nirmal says.

'Can I do everything with this medicine? I mean . . .'

'You can be active,' Nirmal says. 'In fact, you must. At least two hours walking. And you can eat everything.'

I think of the rule about not eating before swimming. I wonder why I'm thinking that.

'Bye, Doctor, thank you so much.'

'Any time, dear.'

I slip out of the door and I look at my phone. Only twenty minutes. I wonder why I'm paying for the hour. And by 'I', I mean 'Amma.'

I pay and pick up my medicines.

Look how seamless these transactions are. How very in control of my life I am.

I feel detached: like I'm administering help to somebody who isn't me. Usually, I'm fine with this. But I wonder what it would be like to actually just feel something for once. *My heart aches, and a drowsy numbness pains my sense . . .*

When I get home, I see Appa sitting on the landing outside the house, in just his white banian and linen shorts. In front of him are spread boot polish, sponges stolen from hotels and five formal pairs of shoes—wingtips, tasselled loafers, brogues, Oxfords.

'Um,' I say. 'What are you doing?'

'Polishing my shoes. How was the doctor? Sam. Sam!'

Sam runs out, still in her school uniform. 'What, Pa?'

'Get me a rag.'

'It was fine. I mean, we only spent like ten minutes together. Oh also, she played a Kishore Kumar song.'

Amma wanders outside, still in her black kurta and big silver necklace, and sits down on the steps. 'Which song?' she asks.

'*Lena hoga janam hume . . .*' I half-sing.

'*Kai kai baar,*' Amma says. 'Shekar, remember? Oh God. What polish is this?'

'All polish smells the same, Hema,' Appa says. 'Ami, you know what we all loved on campus? Hema, what was that song?'

'What song?' Amma asks.

Sam slips her hand into mine. 'What was the diagnosis?'

'Anxiety and depression. But only mild. Gave me medicine.' I stare down at my sandals. I need to re-polish my toenails. Sam lays her head on my shoulder.

'*Appadi.* How suddenly?' Appa asks.

'What do you mean, "how", Shekar. It's not cholera,' Amma stares down at him.

'So what medication is it? Tell me, I'll look it up,' Appa says.

'No, Pa,' Sam objects. 'Please, I don't want you telling her any creepy side effects.'

'If it's liver damage, organ failure, something, we shouldn't know?' Appa asks.

'It's like the tiniest dose ever, Pa, nobody is getting liver damage,' I say. 'Nirmal knows what she's doing.'

'Nothing. Doesn't know what she's doing. Came and nicely told Thatha he had depression. He didn't have depression. He had a sodium-level problem because of those jokers at the hospital. Get me a rag, someone.'

'Of course, of course. Psychiatrists are wrong, doctors are wrong, but only you are right,' Amma says. She hands Appa a rag torn from an old undershirt.

*

18

One day, when Thatha was in the hospital, Amma packed jam sandwiches. Thick, white bread, smeared with rich purple, mixed-fruit, fly-sweet jam, squidging through the slices. She wrapped all the sandwiches in tinfoil, and put them in a Tupperware box, and put the box into her handbag. In her handbag, still, was a Chesapeake Bay book by Nora Roberts.

Thatha had brought the book home one day after his walk and it was sitting on the coffee table. *Don't tell Amma, it's a surprise!*

Amma picked me up. I was at Hindi tuition class. We went to the hospital. The clerk at the surgery recovery ward didn't let her in with the sandwiches. A nurse in civil clothes, at the end of her shift, came up to the clerk after he gestured at her. 'No, madam, you can't.'

'What do you mean I can't,' Amma said. 'He wanted them. You people feed him water instead of sambar. Paper instead of idli. Ami, hold this.'

I held the Tupperware box. It was still warm with Amma's grip. It was bright yellow, indignant, like flowers against the bleak grey of the ward. It smelled like bathrooms, the whole hospital. I hated it. Outside there were hoardings of sapphire peacocks, thick gold chokers, for the jewellery shop on CP Ramaswamy Road. My eyes burnt and I wondered if I had conjunctivitis or something. I wished I did. I wished I were sick and that I was in the hospital instead and that Thatha was home, helping Sam with homework, fighting with Amma about dinner menus again.

I hadn't even broken a stupid arm yet.

I felt useless.

'The full hospital is filled with infections. One jam sandwich won't make any difference,' Amma said. Her kurta had vertical stripes. She smelled like old cotton bedsheets. I couldn't hold her hand—I was too old. But I moved as close to her as I could.

The nurse, Mariam, didn't care about us. 'Sixty patients on this floor, madam,' she said. 'We cannot help everyone with special rules.'

Mariam disappeared behind the counter. Amma frowned at me. 'Walk,' she said. 'Fast. Don't talk.'

Before anyone could stop us, we broke into Room 131. Thatha was asleep. At his bedside were pale red roses wrapped in polka-dotted wrapper; some used tissues; a blood pressure machine; some empty Bisleri bottles; get-well-soon cards with disgustingly lurid, Harpic-blue waterfalls at places he would not see.

Amma hid the Tupperware under Thatha's Indian Railways-brown hospital blanket. He opened his eyes.

'Aha, jam sandwich,' he said.

'Keep quiet, Maama, they're making a fuss,' Amma said. 'Ami, watch the door.'

Mariam walked in and Thatha sat up and folded his arms. 'Hello, Mariam. How are you today?'

'Good, sir, how are you?'

'Fine, very fine.'

'Checking doctor sheet,' Mariam said. She looked at the clipboard near the window.

'All good? Madam brought tiffin, is it?' Mariam asked.

'What tiffin will I eat, ma, where do I have energy for eating anything,' Thatha said, holding up his hands.

The nurse left the room. Thatha reached for the box and Amma opened it for him.

'*Appadi*,' he said. Amma laughed. He picked up a sandwich and Amma sat on the guest chair, holding her handbag close. Thatha gave Amma half and kept half. They both ate.

*

19

Later in the evening, I swallow my medicine and lie down, waiting to see if something big will happen to me. Or has it already happened? Nothing tingling, no cryogenic tomb, nothing taking me over like a fog or a vision . . . Sam floats in to say goodnight, wearing pyjamas with owls whizzing across them.

'Sammy,' I look at her. 'Am I supposed to feel different?'

'Not right now, but it'll help you balance out your moods over time because of the chemicals,' she says wisely. She sits down on my bed. 'Want to listen to a song? Nothing sad.' She talks about the song, *something something new release something something soft something didn't like at first something something*. I suddenly buzz back to the moment and feel guilty for not listening. Sam, flickering, glowing face, floating. Tiny and live wire and sparkly.

'I think I'll sleep off,' I say.

Sam slips out like a shadow and I'm alone. I feel the full weight of the noise in my head. I cover my head with my pillow. I lean back against my bed.

I once asked Amma when I was fifteen: *You know that voice in your head that tells you all your thoughts? Whose voice is that?*

Is that the same voice now? I fall asleep, not intentionally. I haven't remembered to brush my teeth or change out of my 'outside' T-shirt. It happens suddenly, just as I'm wondering if I will ever sleep again.

*

20

Day Five. The parking lot, the tops of frangipani trees, the basketball court. There's a movement, a breeze through the lowest gap between the open glass-pane window and sill, the open latch creating a triangle of air. The sun is soaring high, hidden behind clouds, so the table gets all the light of the sun and none of its menace. Deeksha, Lavanya and Sam hold my worksheets, titled 'Memory'. The poem today is 'I'm Getting Old Now' by Robert Kroetsch. Akshita has not yet arrived in the room.

'So,' I say. 'In this poem, he writes about his mother, and a very specific and random memory comes to him. "We were standing in the garden, or maybe we were kneeling."'

Deeksha takes Lavanya's poetry textbook. 'Because he is old, he remembers certain memories more clearly than others. It's always your own experience that affects how you see the world.'

'My memory is already fading,' Lavanya says. 'I don't even remember class 3 or class 4 properly.'

'We were so different back then, no,' Sam says. 'And sometimes you think you remember one thing but actually remember something else.'

'I want you to write something that plays on that, or that acknowledges it,' I explain. 'Even if it's clear that the character doesn't remember things. Like, see my Casio. Who knows why random things stick in our heads?'

'Show us your poem,' Lavanya says.

'It's not a poem, but here.' I open my notebook and show them my latest essay draft:

For years since Thatha died, images came back to me, like half-remembered dreams that you are so sure morning will keep safe. Then they all ran out, one by one, like cats through an open door.

One day, my sister and I were dancing to a song on the keyboard and Thatha walked in. His footsteps were slow and shuffling, and his hands were behind his back. His shoulders were bent. A towel lay around his shoulders: rich pink, faded now, with a green border. He sat down and we pressed pause.

I didn't know what to say, how to say it . . .

Lavanya keeps her eyebrow raised. 'Then?'

I sigh. 'That's all.'

'You haven't even changed it since last time?' Sam asks. She shakes her head in a disapproving manner. Very few things bother Sam as much as a lack of efficiency.

'Be happy it's shorter than the last version,' I say. 'Okay, give me your critical notes.'

'All depends on what you're trying to put out there,' Deeksha says. 'What are you trying to convey? Is it about suspending a memory in time?'

'You should add your feelings now when you look back at the memory,' Lavanya says. 'I love the "cats running out".'

I picture the half-shadowy hall, during the funeral. Something on the other side of the hall—it was empty, just the key rack, the landing, the staircase and the front door. But it seemed, in the yellow emptiness, like somebody was there. I could almost picture Thatha with his blue shirt, walking in, leaning against the wall to take off his slippers.

'I think I just don't know how he felt,' I say.
I tap my fingers against the desk, cool against my skin.

'But you just said the "Getting Old" poem is about his perspective, how he saw the world.' Lavanya looks up at me.

'Yeah . . . You know, the problem is that it's been a while since all these things happened, too,' I add.

'So why do you still remember them?'

'It just feels important.'

'Why?' Lavanya tilts her head back and smiles, happy at this assessment.

'And half-remembered things can still be good,' Deeksha said. 'Like this Crow-esh, Crochet . . . Robert fellow's poem.'

I nod.

Deeksha clears her throat. 'Okay, I'm going to use this opportunity to sidetrack . . . Can I say something unrelated? Sam, I told Sharon about Akshita.'

'What! Deeksha!' Sam's chair creaks as she turns to look at Deeksha.

'Sorry! It's just that you weren't doing anything about it and Akshita . . . Ami, Akshita's been even more sad lately and I know she's not talking to her mom or anything . . . And she's going to talk to Sharon now . . . I didn't tell Sharon Akshita wanted to HURT herself, but I said something to the effect of she was sad.'

'Oh God, oh God.' Sam bends her head and holds her head in her hands. 'This is going to become a big thing. I didn't want it to be *anything*. She's going now?'

'Yeah. They said after school in the free period today. Which ... Is now,' Deeksha says. 'I'm sorry, Sam ... I waited and waited for you to do something and you didn't do anything.'

'It's okay, it's okay,' Sam says, almost to herself. She holds Deeksha's hands, which are stretched out on the table, waiting for Sam to do something: hold them or push them away or something. Sam leans forward and tries to recompose herself. 'It's just that this wasn't part of my plan,' she mumbles.

At this point, it sounds like Sam is talking to herself; she is looking past us. 'I just thought it was Akshita's problem to sort out and I shouldn't interfere. You have to compartmentalize. Nothing else you can do.'

Lavanya, who had been listening to all this silently and all-knowingly, stops swivelling her chair. She leans forward. 'Sam is even less confrontational than me. She has her own weird way of dealing with everything.'

'Sam, don't be angry, dude. I was scared for Akshita.' Deeksha tries to explain.

'I'm not, I'm not . . . I'm just thinking about what to do,' Sam mumbles again, and squeezes Deeksha's hands. She stands up.

I am still contemplating my response to all this when Sam calls me.

'Ami?'

'Mm?'

'Can you come?' She stands, wavering before me.

'That might be good.' Deeksha nods approvingly. 'She's a neutral presence.'

Sam and I walk to the principal's office. The campus is all empty, the way it looks in dreams: the same places, but without anyone in them, silent oil paintings. The rain has turned everything wet, soft. The field stretches before us, the canteen glimmers, a few cars are parked on the side roads like sleeping beasts. The haze of the sand seems to hang in the air. The rainy winter is spreading: some sweat in this early evening but less than usual, and a light breeze, a light drizzle of rain. Sam doesn't speak, and I know she doesn't want to speak—her hands are clenched into fists.

We reach the office, where Michael is nowhere to be found, and Akshita is sitting on the highly uncomfortable black plastic chair. Her uniform shirt is loose on her and she has done the thing KGM girls do, folding up and shortening the sleeves with a perfect cuff. Her face looks bare, like she has come here mid-sleep. Instead of her usual 'at the edge' sort of precarious energy, today she is drooping, her arms slumped near her knees. She takes up all the space on the chair as she spills on to it: a slowly deflating bouncy house.

She doesn't seem surprised to see Sam. I try to linger in a discreet manner near the bamboo blinds.

'Hi,' Akshita says. She tilts her chin towards Sharon's office. 'Thought I might as well finish it off.'

'Can I come?' Sam asks.

'Yeah, she'll anyway ask to see you too.'

'And Ami is here,' Sam says, without offering further context.

Akshita looks at me. 'Hi, Ami.'

'Hi.'

The door opens, and Michael—there he is—raises his eyebrows, unsurprised to see me. 'Come,' he says. Sam and Akshita walk in and I take one step forward, sunlight falling on my shin.

'What,' Michael says. 'You'll stand here only?'

'How are you, Michael?'

'Go quick inside. All of you.'

I walk in. Sharon looks up from reading Michael's famous register.

'Hello, Ami.'

'Hi, Ma'am.'

Sam and Akshita sit on the two chairs, opposite Sharon.

'I'll just ask Michael to get a chair—' says Sharon.

'That's really fine, Ma'am, I don't mind, please go ahead.'

'So, girls, you have been feeling upset about something.'

'It's nothing, Ma'am,' Akshita whispers.

Sharon regards them with an imperial look while her salt-and-pepper hair ripples under the fan. 'I understand you had some relationship trouble . . .'

Akshita and Sam seize up and look at each other instead of talking. Akshita folds and unfolds her fingers, creating little tentlike patterns.

Sharon's gaze is firm. 'Do you speak to your family about it?'

'Sometimes,' Akshita says.

Sam looks from Akshita to Sharon. 'Yeah, so do I, I bring it up to my parents sometimes, when it's the *right* time.'

Sam pauses and, outside, Michael yells something out to the grounds staff person, who is pouring fresh chalk dust on the field to create wide concentric circles within its perimeter.

'All right, Akshita, you've been upset, withdrawn, according to teachers and peers.' Sharon turns to her. 'You didn't talk to the counsellor . . . Soon class 12 is coming up and you need to be mentally peaceful to approach the year.'

'Ma'am, sorry to interrupt.' It's Sam. 'But no one talks to the counsellor.'

Akshita tilts her head slightly. 'She is very . . . judgemental.'

Sharon nods slowly. 'You could speak to each other? Why do you not? You've been friends since LKG.'

'We do speak, Ma'am, it's not like we don't,' Akshita says. She turns to Sam, who nods.

'And of course, you know I am here,' Sharon says.

Of course, they are both unlikely to take Sharon up on that offer.

'And please do attend Ami's classes. Only two remain, right, Ami?'

'Three more, Ma'am.'

'I will,' Akshita says. 'I mostly do . . . Just sometimes, there's choir or I have tuition. Then there was the model UN last week.' She's lying, but I appreciate the lie.

'I know, it just might be good for you,' Sharon says, taking her spectacles off, rubbing the phantom spots on her nose where the pincers rested. 'Ami, how are the classes?'

'They're great,' Sam says, before I can answer. 'We're writing so much good poetry, Ma'am, we're going to put it all in the *KGM Digest* before the carnival.'

Sharon presses her sari pleats down even though they're already smooth: a pale pink net sari. 'Great. Writing can be useful, cathartic . . . you know. Akshita, please try to attend.'

'Yes, Ma'am.'

They're both sitting on the edge of their seats. Like a balloon bursting, the tension in the room breaks when Sharon pushes back her chair.

'Thank you, girls, and if there is anything else, please do not hesitate. Akshita, please come meet me again before the holidays.'

'Yes, Ma'am.'

We leave the room and Akshita raises her eyebrows at Sam. 'My God, I'm so tired. I'm going to get some sour marbles. Then I'm going home. I'll see you on . . .'

'Tomorrow and then on Thursday if you're coming for the writing class,' Sam says.

Akshita turns around and looks at us, even as she is walking away. 'I'll come.'

Sam and I look at each other gravely. Sam's skirt hangs loose on her, her eyes sparkling behind her spectacles.

'That was . . . a Thing!' Sam exclaims.

'Was it? You guys barely discussed anything.'

'It was a *lot* if you read subtext, Ami.'

I burst out laughing. 'My mistake.'

We walk back towards the library. 'Want sour marbles?' I ask Sam.

'Fine,' Sam says.

We make a quick pitstop at the canteen for sour marbles—Michael says I can pay him later—and we eat as we walk. I take all the green marbles; Sam takes all the tamarind-flavoured ones. We leave the poor, orange-flavoured ones in the bottom of the packets. We can't even eat them out of pity.

'You know something?' Sam says. 'Apparently, Akshita cried on the phone again the other day and told Deeksha she was feeling depressed and might do something . . . like hurt herself or something, and she wanted Deeksha to stay with her on the phone. And then Deeksha said she was so scared something would happen to Akshita, and she said she would tell me; Akshita said not to, then she said she'd tell Akshita's mom, she said no to that too. Then she said maybe she would tell Sharon . . .'

'But she didn't hurt herself, right?' I ask Sam.

'No, no, luckily,' Sam gestures with a green sour marble, 'But Deeksha said, what if she did? So she told Sharon . . . Anyway, I'm glad she told me. You know, Akshita's new "friends",' Sam said with air quotes, 'in Commerce are so useless. That's why Deeksha keeps calling to check on her. I would call too, but I don't know. It's easier to stay updated through Deeksha . . . I don't know,' Sam says. 'Anyway, she won't talk to me, so it's nice to stay updated through Deeksha at least.'

'Poor Akshita,' I say.

'*What?*' Sam stops, mid-marble chew, near the parking lot. 'Ami, you're supposed to be on *my* side.'

'Sam. Obviously I am . . .' I squeeze her arm, soft and bendy. She hugs me back and moves away quickly.

'Righto,' Sam says as we return to the table. Lavanya is half-asleep on top of her Salinger. Deeksha is flipping through a Horrible Histories about the British Empire; the kids' shelf in the corner is filled with them.

'How was it, how was it, how was it? Tell me everything right now,' Deeksha says, jumping in her seat.

'Actually, it was okay. We managed Sharon. Now we have to just monitor the situation,' Sam says.

Lavanya perks up and taps at the book. 'Okay, for once let's talk about something besides Akshita. Ami, I have an idea—what do you think of this . . .' Lavanya says. She sits up straighter in her chair and stretches out her arms. Her braid swishes over her uniform shirt. 'Maybe this time we can try looking at a book we like, something that's not in the syllabus. We'll just bring a book and talk. I'll talk about this one.' She taps her book. 'These short stories.'

'I love that,' Deeksha says. 'It'll motivate us to finally read properly.'

'Great idea, it'll be interesting to see what you like reading and maybe if you can apply stuff from this class too,' I say. 'Okay, so for now, let's just write about a thing we remember, or half-remember.'

Deeksha unclicks her Lexi pen and taps it against her temple, swaying right, left. 'My first day of school,' she says. 'I begged my mom to let me decide my own hairstyle, but she made me wear two ponytails. And every day when I came to school, I would go to the bathroom, take the ponytails out, and retie my hair. I don't know why I remember that. I was like six.'

'Oh my God, me too!' Lavanya's voice is ultrasonic; she reaches out and squeezes Deeksha's arm. 'I was six, and I was going to Kodaikanal with my mom, and we were going up this really steep hill, hairpin bend, everything, and I suddenly had this thought. It just came to me. What if we just fell? And my mom's like, this is exactly what you're not supposed to think when you're driving up a literal hill.' Laughter fills the room like fireflies.

You would not believe your eyes if ten million fireflies lit up the world as I fell asleep.

'I'm thinking of Annual Day,' Sam says, 'but it's a bit sad.'

'Which Annual Day?'

'Seven years ago,' Sam says.

'So like class 5?'

'Class 4.' Sam rubs her right arm with her left hand. She breathes in. 'Do you remember? I'm sure you guys don't even remember. We wore those red sequined skirts, those big red scrunchies, and we were dancing to that Hrithik Roshan song. Remember, Lavanya, you were also in it.'

'Oh God. I blocked it out,' Lavanya says. 'And that bright red lipstick as blush.'

'So I ask my mom to come and watch, and my granddad was sick that day, like he was at home—we thought maybe he'd need to go to the hospital, but then she promised me she would come. My dad wasn't in town and Ami was like, I'll go myself, but my mom wanted to come. So she came, and then my granddad got sick suddenly in the night and had to be taken to the hospital and everything, in an ambulance. He ended up staying all night and then you know, the next day . . . That was his last day.' Sam chokes up: but she clears her throat, keeps talking, steady voice. 'I remember I was just sitting there in that stupid skirt, the sequins were so cheap that there was glitter all over our hands and legs, and lipstick on my face. My mom was stuck there too.'

A tiny Sam on the stage, with her cheeks still red, the skies turning grey, the insides of the auditorium grey, all the rich charcoal grey of my memory, a cavernous space, her bangles still jingling.

There's a small silence now creeping into the room, like a moth fluttering at the edges of the wall. But Deeksha and Lavanya know what to do. This is the ephemeral world they know, which I know in my own way too. They hug Sam, and she hugs them back: they're a single, kindly monster-creature of limbs and half-ponytails.

Like it's been waiting all this time for a quiet moment, my body starts hurting. I can feel a numbness, like wet paint, spread through my arms, down my neck.

'Build on these,' I say, with a heroic calm. 'And don't try and remember every detail—play on what you do remember and leave in the gaps, like Kroetsch did. And like Lavanya is saying, it'll be interesting to add your present-day self in the poem, who's looking at all of this happen.'

They look out of the window, at the shelf in the distance, at the plywood table surface. They write, the pens scratching on their ruled paper, and I start to get up, slowly, as they are still talking.

'Sam lost so much weight that year,' Lavanya says.

'Really?' Deeksha looks at Sam.

'Yeah, yeah.' Lavanya nods. 'I have this photo of us at the carnival that year. You can see the bones on her elbow and her ribs.'

'That's not true,' Sam says. 'It was a growth spurt.'

'Don't lie!'

I slip out of the room, too tired to ask them to write instead of talk. I ache with the weight of Sam's words, in places I didn't know I could feel. My ankles, my neck, my mind. Sometimes I wonder what would happen to me if I actually ran a marathon because just this conversation makes me tired. My heart feels deflated but my heartbeat is as loud as the bass drum that some class 11 student used to play, balancing it on an old MRF tyre, during march-past practice.

That day, right after the Annual Day, Amma had dropped Sam home and then gone to the hospital. Sam and I kept the landline on our bed, in between both of our pillows, waiting for the phone to ring. I finally fell asleep by eleven in the night, but Sam sat awake, still in her make-up and her red skirt, on the computer chair near the window. The night turned indigo. She sat with her knees drawn to her chest, staring out of the window, her shoulders tense and alert.

*

21

We are lying on the bed, looking up at the green stars on my ceiling. Sam is rubbing Nivea into my temples and pressing my head. I've had little twinges of headaches and shoulder aches.

'Did you take your medicine?' Sam asks me. 'How do you feel?'

'Don't say medicine and all. It makes me feel so . . . Not normal.'

'But you *are* not normal.'

I whack Sam's hand. 'Press, press, don't get distracted.'

Sam kneads my head gently. 'She's coming now,' Sam says gravely.

'Who?'

'Akshita. She wants some notes. Open the door when it rings.'

'You open the door, she's your friend.'

'She's *not*.'

Time passes and I'm half-asleep. Then, I wake up: Sam has stopped pressing. The doorbell rings. Sam sits straight. My head starts to tingle again.

'Open the *door*, Ami.'

I run down the stairs. Akshita stands there, sparkling in navy, and Siddharth is next to her. She automatically leans towards him. I think of plants at a window stretching towards the sun.

'Hey, guys, come in,' I say. The running has got my head feeling all electric. I feel dull twinges in my skull, like marbles are clacking against its walls. I shut my eyes against the pressure, frowning. Akshita and Siddharth shuffle in. Akshita contemplates whether to leave her Clarks sandals in the hall or walk in with them. Siddharth looks up at the painting: a tapestry of the churning of the ocean.

'I'm sorry, I have this headache. Can I get you guys anything? Something to eat or . . .? We have Arun ice cream. Butterscotch.'

'No, Ami, that's fine.' Siddharth smiles. 'We're just here to pick up the notes. Maths, no, Aksh?'

'Yeah, Sam's tuition notes,' Akshita says. 'From last week.'

Are they together or not at this point of time? I have this vague thought in my head, but it doesn't seem my place to ask. I walk to the stairs and holler at Sam to come downstairs with the notes.

In one quick flurry, Sam runs downstairs and gives Akshita the notes, and then they all walk towards the front door. They talk until the door shuts, their voices getting lower and lower. I busy myself by entering the kitchen, rearranging the fridge magnets and trying not to listen.

The last sound is of laughter as Akshita leaves.

Sam rematerializes in the kitchen.

'Best friends again? You were all chatty,' I tell Sam.

'Oh, come on, Ami,' Sam waves this idea away. She slides on to the kitchen counter.

'We stopped being friends in class 9 itself, when we were in different sections and Akshita made other friends. So that's when I learnt.'

'What did you learn?'

'People are who they are. You have to be smart and *adapt*. And *obviously* I'm not saying you shouldn't forgive people; you should, but only from a safe distance. That's why I became friends with Deeksha and became friends again with Lavanya. I had to spread out my options, you know, have different friends for different things.'

'This is all so Darwinian.'

Sam shrugs. 'I'm just being *honest*, that's how friendship actually is.'

'So this is what you meant? That day? You said you have to save everything, you're all alone, everyone is asleep and you're so pressured?'

'Noo, Ami, I wasn't talking about that . . .' Sam turns to me suddenly like she's scared I'll hear. What's she going to say? I wait a moment. She recalibrates. Her pupils return to normal size; her shoulders un-tense themselves.

'Okay, so to be *fully* honest . . . Yeah, it stresses me out, but . . . Family stuff stresses me out more.' Sam squeezes my hands like she is spreading a current into them.

'You mean me?'

'Yeah, sometimes you.' Sam looks at me, eyes darting and wary. 'But only sometimes.'

I feel a shock so sudden, my head stops hurting. Like a loud air cooler finally stopping its whirring: a quiet settling. I think of all the messages she sent me when I was in college: *Now what are u doing? Did u change? Get breakfast? It's okay, go in your pyjamas and wear your coat. Why were u awake so early?* All the evenings when I was lying in bed, and she appeared at my door, holding her toothbrush, frowning against the light, her hair clinging to my doorframe with static: *Now how are you feeling? And now?*

'You can tell me, Sammy, if you're worried about me.' I turn to her. 'I would be worried about me.'

'Not now, not any more,' Sam says. 'I *was* worried a month ago. You just seemed stressed, even after we talked and I cheered you up . . . And I know you didn't even tell Alicia or Amma how sad you were. And I didn't want to tell Amma. I used to worry about you *all* the time. Even in my dreams.'

Sam plays with the skin of an orange, slowly unpeeling it. She holds it out towards me: *Want?* I shake my head and lean back against the fridge: *No, you keep it.* She eats an orange slice, looking into the distance, that half-frown back.

I look at myself like I am out of my body. It's like I've been fighting against this fog, like the fog of mosquito fumigation smoke, and I can't fight it, it's everywhere. Imagine trying to understand me all the way from Chennai. Everything looks so stark suddenly. The blue-white of the kitchen wall, under the flickering tube light. The orange floor. The comforting feeling of the countertop against my back. Everything is so small and simple. Imagine Sam, coming home, leaving her bag next to the shoe rack, running up the stairs . . . Watching TV and then when it's five o'clock, checking her phone: *Ami must be awake.* And what did they talk about? Sam, Amma, Appa, sitting at the table, without me?

Amma: 'Maybe it's time for Ami to come home.'

Sam looking from Appa to Amma, plucking off tiny pieces of her roti: *How much should I tell them?*

What if they just wanted an elder sister/daughter who had funny college stories? About rowing team or the dean's list or the friend-group trip to get sushi or fried chicken after exams? Like everyone else had? And I didn't for some reason.

Is that what I thought college would be, when I picked the college that didn't need tests and was not ridiculously expensive for Amma and Appa? And when did it all change for me? Was it on the flight, somewhere over the Zagros mountains, like a slowly leaking bag of wheat: a grain, a grain, everything gone? Was it the first night when I tiptoed over my flatmate's Jenga-stack of unwashed dishes to go into my room and sleep on my bed? Was it the first time I looked out of the window during Introduction to Qualitative Research, and saw the poky branches of the ash tree and the thick orange leaves, like palms, clatter against the window, and looked back at the whiteboard and had no idea what I'd missed?

Or was it before that, in class 12, when Alicia had left school and I roamed around alone, finally relaxing at the end of the day when Sam and I got into our carpool? Or was it when I spent one month in class 8 watching *Friends* DVDs instead of going to school and Appa said, 'How much longer will you let this happen,' and Amma said, 'What would you suggest and plus she went to school on Monday, I'm just saying one more day . . .'

Did Sam remember all this? Did she tally my life decisions and actions like they were marks in a game of Scrabble? How far back did everyone's memory go? Did everyone remember what I remembered? Did I remember correctly?

It's like it's settling on me now, dust after a hot desert storm: how much everyone has felt because of me, which I selfishly never thought about because I was living through the moment, instead of looking at it from every angle. How much do I owe Sam and have owed Sam, and how much do I still have to pay back? It's like half of Sam's world is with me, moving slowly with my every moment, like the earth and the moon, sapping Sam's energy, leaving her hands empty.

'Are you okay?' Sam asks.

A multiple-choice question.

'Yeah. Should we go watch TV?'

'Can I choose?' Sam asks.

'Fine.'

We leave the kitchen and I see Sam's shoulders hunch as she squeezes past the fridge. Mentally, I take my half out of my hands and put it back with Sam's half—give her the whole world back.

*

22

I feel half-deflated before the next doctor's appointment. I don't even have time to prepare a script in my head, plan out exactly what I'll say. I weakly spray some body mist against my shirt and under my arms. I can't focus on my own thoughts because my family is extremely vocal in airing theirs.

Amma: 'Listen, let me come. Last time also you didn't.'

She's putting on her socks and shoes, all set to go for a walk. She wears her oldest, loosest blue T-shirt, fraying at the neck, and purple capri pants.

Appa: 'First, explain clearly what's even wrong with you. I just don't understand. Why does nobody explain anything properly?'

Sam: 'Appa, she already has and even I have.'

Appa deliberately forgets everything I tell him. I really do not have the patience for Appa right now. He's like that last book you place on a teetering pile that brings the whole thing down.

Me: 'Appa, I already told you . . .'

Appa: 'Sorry it's so inconvenient to repeat yourself.'

Me: 'No, I'm not saying . . .'

Appa: 'No, leave it. Please don't bother.'

First moment of silence of the day: at Nirmal's office. Amma ends up dropping me off and I am so preoccupied that I only feel guilty once I'm alone in the waiting room.

Text message: *Sorry u had to drop me!!!*

In her office, Nirmal is typing on her phone, using just her index fingers. She waves at me with the phone when I enter.

'No music this time?' I ask.

'What's that, dear?'

'The music. I liked it.'

'Oh, of course, dear, some patients don't like it. But I don't switch it off, I simply reduce the volume.'

She points, with her fingers and eyebrows, at the small stereo on the shelf above the CCTV camera. I turn the volume dial: another mellow song.

Tum hi toh layi ho jeevan mein mere, pyaar, pyaar, pyaar.

'How do you children type so fast?' she asks. 'I am trying out this phone to talk to my niece. It is very challenging. Present from a patient. Usually, they just present a sweet box or some flowers.'

Thanks for saving my life, here, have an iPhone. Have some doodh pedas. It's all so horrifying. I sit down.

150

The stool is rough and plastic, and totters on one leg. The floor has grey flecks painted into the squares of tile.

'How are we doing?' Nirmal asks.

'Great,' I say.

'Why don't we define "great"?'

The phenomenon due to which . . . Due to high fluid content, the cell is in a state of . . . Impossible to answer these questions.

'Just good, fairly calm,' I say.

'How many good days, if you would like to define it as such, or normal days, if you prefer that, have you had?'

Finally, some answers. Or wait, I have to answer. She looks at me, her eyebrows raised.

Answer the question, Ami.

'Mostly happy,' I say. I switch off the part of my brain that will actually analyse that response. Nothing majorly unhappy has happened, so that must mean happiness.

Right?

Kehna hai, kehna hai . . .

'And if I have to ask about your tiredness? Appetite?'

'All good.'

'Fantastic. And you are walking every day?'

'Yes, I walk home from school, where I work, sometimes, or just in the evenings when it's not raining.'

'Your road is nice to walk on,' Nirmal says. 'Sometimes I pack my walking shoes and water bottle in the car, drive to Adyar, just to walk there. But it's raining too much these days.'

'Coming from Kochi, right?' I ask her, as if I know enough about pressure systems.

'I think from the north, dear, it is raining cats and dogs in Delhi, Bangalore also, everywhere. Tell me, any anger, any sleeplessness?'

'No.'

'Everything fine with family?'

'All good.'

'And they are supportive as you are dealing with your situation and your diagnosis?' Nirmal asks, looking over her spectacles at her prescription pad.

'Yeah, my mom, my dad, everyone.'

'All right, very good.' Nirmal scribbles on her prescription pad. I wonder how many people are waiting outside. The camera doesn't cover everyone. I look up at the ceiling, and next to the Ajanta clock is a sepia portrait of a man. He has wavy hair and his head is tilted to the side, as if to say, 'Don't lie to me.' He has a sharp nose and looks like Jinnah or Nehru.

'Great photo,' I say, pointing up.

Nirmal turns slowly, looking not directly at the portrait but to its side.

'My husband,' she says. 'It has been ten years.'

'I'm sorry,' I say. I really mean it. It isn't a generic space-filler. Does she know that?

'Thank you, dear.' She looks at the portrait. 'He loved that portrait. Asked for it in sepia, even though studios had well moved into colour. What a stubborn man.' She laughs, a slow chuckle, a dripping tap. 'You see the locked door, by the reception?'

'Yes?'

'His office.' Nirmal stops writing and looks up, pen still in hand. 'Did you make a list of the unanswerable questions you have?'

'Oh, that. I think so.' I did make a list on my phone, in that timeless space between night and morning, the light shining hollow in my room. But I don't know how it'll sound aloud. 'Do you want me to read them?'

She holds up her hands. 'Of course, anything that will give me an insight into your mind, how you look at everything around you.'

'Sure, one second.' I open my phone.

'Okay so:

Why do we die?

What happens if all the songs and compositions in the world run out, how will A.R. Rahman think of new tunes?

How long are you supposed to feel sad when someone dies? Have I overshot it?'

Nirmal turns a little bit towards me, her face like a bird with a sharp beak, waiting.

'About my granddad,' I say. 'It made me so sad. And everyone else got over it.'

'Got over?'

'You know. Processed.'

Nirmal smiles and taps her pen on her prescription pad. 'Of course, everyone has to process a loss, and everyone processed the loss of your grandfather. But you should look at the stages of your emotional journey. So what if the process takes one year or . . .' She closes her eyes to think. 'Has it been seven years?'

'I think so.'

'Sometimes I cannot believe it.' She turns her chair, points at the portrait of her husband. 'Look at Anil. I lost him ten years ago. And just the other day, I met his brother, who has "processed" it, as you say. But I noticed he was buying lauki. Now this is a vegetable he hates. I asked him why. He said he started buying it so long ago that now he can't stop. Anil was very fond of lauki, you know. He said he never thinks about Anil on a daily basis, until he is buying vegetables, and then it just happens. What do you think about that?'

We live in that moment of silence—or as long as we can before we remember where we are. Nirmal, of course, is looking at the CCTV camera with the number of people (four) waiting outside.

I look at my notebook.

'Can I just ask you one more question?'

'Ask away, dear.'

'Will I always have this?'

'This . . .'

'This condition.'

Take it back. Whatever it is.

'You will have phases, dear. Sometimes more intense, sometimes less intense,' Nirmal says. She signs her prescription. 'I told your mother, now that you have a routine, it will be great to see a psychologist. I can recommend one for you. And I will write this prescription. No nausea, no dizziness, is that right? Let's continue for a month. You can update me on how you are finding things.'

'Sure.' I consider telling Nirmal about Alicia. I decide to do it fast, given the four people waiting. 'My friend went to a therapist when she was stressed out about studies. I think it was in Ignatius Hospital. Anyway, she was really sweet, listened to her and everything, and then spent fifteen minutes drawing her a study timetable.' I think of Alicia,

155

how she showed me the side of her head. *Look, my hair is falling, I have a bald patch now.*

'And I did go to a counsellor in the UK,' I continue, 'but . . . I still . . .'

I'm still whatever I was.

'Think about it, dear,' Nirmal says. 'You have some time. The full city is slowing down, now that the year is almost over. Look.' She points out at the road: only two parked scooters, one crow poking at a half-full plastic bag with wet rice, the arms of a banyan moving gently. 'See. You have quite some time.'

Nirmal looks at me over the top of her glasses. She taps her hand on the desk. Her veins are—a mild exaggeration—as thick as cement pipes.

'Do not worry, dear,' she says. 'I always say this. Every part of us makes us who we are. You will see that this is one part of you. Just one part. Like your arteries or tendons.'

When I leave the clinic and blink in the fresh light, I imagine my disease—is it a disease?—like my skin, a barrier between me and the world, between raw nerve and fresh air.

Maybe if you say something enough times, it becomes a medical fact rather than the first thing you say when you talk about yourself. Easier to hide. A part of you, but separate. Like a pet dog, with you but not you.

*

23

I walk out quietly. There's a low hum in my head, like a car on idle mode.

Everything seems ten times worse than it is. AMI IS EXAGGERATING! But I just want to be like everyone else for a while. Take up as little space as possible.

I walk up and down on the strip of sand next to the main road, looking for an auto. Cars pass by, motorcycles pass by, autos with full passenger seats pass by, but I just can't find an empty one that will take me home. Past the plant nursery on the main road, a slow drumbeat sounds, followed by a procession of dancing people and, in the very middle of the procession, a tall bamboo throne held up by four people. On the throne is a dead person being paraded through the roads on the way to the crematorium. I stare at him, his eyes shut, cotton wool in his nose, propped up, sitting straight, to look like he is awake. Flower garlands of yellow, green, white, magenta and purple surround his chair, creating a bed of colour. People dance around him, moving with the flow of a river, along with the traffic. The sky curves around them like a dome. The beat seems to be getting louder and louder, until it enters my head and my temples beat with it, every beat slowly pushing apart my temples and skull and the skin that holds my mind in one place.

I need to stop seeing this person's face, staring straight at me from his throne. I want to run, but I can only walk. I slowly turn away from the main road and walk deeper and deeper inside until I reach the park, dotted with a few small children, uncles, municipal workers. I sit on the bench. On the ground in front of me is brick, splattered with white paint, some dried grass and a fallen flower. One municipal worker swings on the children's swings in front of me, grey shirt buttoned over her sari, the swing creaking. Next to her, her broom and wheelbarrow lie against the sand, like they are asleep.

The drumbeats are in my head. Someone knocking, waiting to be let out. Soft thuds against my skin, at my temples. A thump, another thump, another thump. The ground shaking with the bass of the drumbeat. Gone, but still here on the ground of the park.

A faint buzzing comes from my jeans pocket and I realize where I am. Amma calling. Every tick of my brain and my heart and my fingers feels like it's bass-heavy. I answer the phone. Amma is on her evening walk and the shrieks of the traffic puncture the phone line.

'How was it?'

'Ma . . .'

She politely waits as my voice catches up with my thoughts.

Dumdumdumdum DUM dumdumdumdumdumdumdumdum.

It comes slowly. 'She just said to keep having the medicine and apparently, I will always have anxiety and depression.' How simple it sounds now. How very not simple it is.

'Yeah . . .' Amma's voice is unimpressed. She's waiting for a fresh piece of information.

'That's all, Ma, that's the news.'

'Ami, you knew that already.'

'I know, I know, but still. It's just more final, or something. Or I'm just realizing.' I don't say anything more, but I stay on the phone. It's exhausting now, the label of depression or anxiety. Like I always have to prove something. I stare at the windows of the flats surrounding the park, the glimmer of TV screens through them, like windows into windows. Blue squares that stare down at me.

'Are you okay?' Amma asks. She says something else I don't hear. '. . . Told you . . . Should come . . .' Now her voice is clear again. 'Who asked you to go alone?'

A few weeds curl at my toes. That one flower that falls right off the fuzzy stem, if you snap and flick at it. What's it called? The woman on the swing calls out to someone outside the park; the gate creaks; low voices I can't hear even though I am right here. A tan and white dog squeezes through the gate, bounces as he walks on the sand, ears flapping. He turns towards his own tail like he wants to swat it away.

'Come home,' Amma says. 'Come now. I'll come back right away.'

Say something, Ami.

'Okay, Ma. Bye.'

* * *

I find an auto, after long, dripping moments. 'Seventy rupees,' he says once I have sat down, like an afterthought. Because I didn't bother to negotiate or even ask the cost.

Should I have?

Low hums, the sweet-acid smell of car fumes, blaring horn sounds that shake the vinyl of the auto. On the seat in front of me rolls the driver's long, plastic water bottle. The water is probably hot and tastes of plastic.

I listen to more Oasis.

Something hit me somewhere right between the eyes.

I am alone when I get home. The house is completely quiet. Sam and Appa are out; Amma is still on her walk.

I don't have to worry if my smile is wide enough.

You worry about seeming happy to your own family?
What the hell is wrong with you?
I wanna talk tonight until the mornin' light.

I sit in the hall, put on the TV. I watch nothing in particular: just flowers and floating ticker tapes and dancing people and beautifully decorated sets of living rooms that aren't actually being lived in.

I think of J.D. Salinger who said he was in love with a TV star. How he wrote letters that never got answered. I never want to fall in love with something that isn't real, but I don't want to feel real, either.

Head, don't hurt now, please. So boring and predictable.

I slump lower on to the printed-peonies cushion, and the coaster with Amma's face gleaming next to the Rock Temple.

I start to feel the tiredness now, as if years have collapsed into this moment. I have to get out, stand up, but I am simultaneously dripping with a metal-heavy slowness that does not allow me to go anywhere. My head is swimming. A stray dog barks outside and then, or maybe it's connected, a car makes a highly shrill set of cascading beeps as it reverses: to the tune of 'Row, Row, Row Your Boat'.

I am scared. I am scared to take my medicine and scared not to. I'm scared to explain to my parents what Nirmal said and I'm scared about what is going on in my mind and

I wonder if I will ever feel anything again and I wonder who I can talk to and I wonder if I can even talk at all.

'A part of you. Like your arteries or your tendons.' It is here.

My heart is loud and aching in my chest.

Take your stupid medicine.

Two minutes . . .

You and me, see how we are.

The house is making its whistling, quietening sounds: the fuse box and the fridge settling for the night. I slowly adjust my eyes to the darkness.

The low metal door clicks and Amma walks into the house.

'Ami?'

I close my eyes. It hurts to talk, to look at Amma, to look at anything. Amma's voice sounds low, disembodied, hollow and ringing off itself. She walks into the hall, still in her white Nike socks. Sweat glistens at her cheekbones.

I slowly drift back, a paper boat in the rain. Amma slumps down on the sofa.

Talk to her. Think about something other than your own self.

'How was your walk?'

'Good. Still not enough exercise today, but something is better than nothing.' Amma presses her palm against my forehead, like she is checking a temperature.

'You must be feeling tired from having . . .'

'Ma. I just don't want to talk about it. I know it's big and important and all, but I can't bear that look.'

'What look? I don't have a look.'

The room is pale, lit only by the half-asleep TV. But I see Amma's look: big eyes, a frown, slightly teary.

'You do,' I say.

Amma clears her face, a typically Amma swift gesture: like she has turned on the windshield wipers when it has just started to drizzle.

'Don't move, I'm coming,' Amma says.

She walks into her bathroom to shower and returns in less than five minutes, wearing her bright blue nightie. She smells like sweet shampoo and sharp perfume.

'Here,' Amma says. 'We should have a drink.'

'No, Ma.'

'Come on. A proper one. Wait.'

Amma swans out and back into the room and keeps a half-drunk bottle of red wine and two glasses on the coffee table. She pours. The liquid glistens perfectly dark, perfectly bubbly.

I take a sip. At first, it's bitter. Then, it spreads inside me like a cosy fire.

Amma half-sits, half-lies down on the sofa, looking at her phone.

'I'm assuming you don't want to chat?' she says.

We drink in silence, and it slowly gets darker outside. All the purple evening light has vanished, leaving only darkness. Amma turns on the lamps near the sofa. She is like Florence Nightingale.

*

24

The second sip of wine is less strong; sweeter.

'You like it?' Amma asks. 'This is a nice wine.'

'It's nicer than that Tesco wine,' I tell her. 'Remember? In . . .' *College?*

'Hello, Tesco wine is amazing,' Amma says. 'You remember we bought Tesco wine and came back to my lodge room, I bought a plastic glass also and I drank when you went to that party?'

Amma is talking about the first week when I was at college. She was there for the first two weeks, staying in a lodge with sloping roofs, and orange-juice breakfasts in the arboretum. One of the nights—it would get dark by 6 p.m.—there was a party in my hostel, Pizza and Barbecue Night. I promised Amma I would go and try and talk to some people. I didn't go.

'Ma, I never went to that.'

'What do you mean you never went,' Amma says. She sits up straighter on the sofa, takes a sip of her wine. 'You left my room, no?'

'I did. But then I was tired. I just went to my room and lay there.'

Amma tilts her head back to take another sip. When she keeps the glass back down, she is still looking at me.

'Why, ma,' Amma says. 'I was right there. You should have told me if you wanted company.' She leans forward and reaches her arm out. The coffee table separates us. I can't move: it's like I'm melted into the ground, like hot plastic. I stretch my feet on the ten-year-old Kashmiri carpet.

'I didn't want to disturb you. But I felt so bad I wasn't spending time with you,' I say. 'I was just too tired to even talk to you.'

'I wanted you to make friends,' Amma says. 'You told me you went to that bar, Duke of Cambridge?'

'I lied. I got that name from my flatmate, the one you met, tall, with the socks and Adidas sandals.'

Amma frowns at me and then starts to laugh.

'I'm so sorry, Ma,' I say.

Amma is still laughing. 'It's okay. You wanted to be alone, so you went to your room.' Amma takes another sip. 'How is it?'

I can't bear picturing Amma alone in her lodge room, the tiny white bed, the sloping ceiling, the plastic cup of wine, the vegetable crisps, the half-open suitcase with her black cardigan strewn across it.

But now I'm laughing too.

I take a sip, the soft purple hitting every pipe inside my throat.

'Okay, Ma, your turn. Put a song, anything you want.'

I shut my eyes. Amma chooses a Bruce Springsteen song.

Sometimes it's like someone took a knife, baby, edgy and dull.

Amma sips her wine and holds her hand out to me. Indents of knife handles, hair oil, laundry detergent, Nivea Soft, all on her palm.

We drink some wine.

A freight train running through the middle of my head.

The song goes on and Amma opens her laptop. I bring my own laptop out to get through my essay readings, and open a biography on Jibanananda Das, little highlights still gleaming from when I had last marked up the book. My eyes are slow to process. But now, it seems easier to read that one page. Why had this stupid thing taken me weeks in college? I highlight this poem excerpt:

There is some other perilous wonder
Which frolics
In our very blood.

I feel myself getting full with the words. After half a chapter, I look up and Amma isn't looking at her laptop any more. She has fallen into a light sleep, curled on the sofa. I poke her, until she opens her eyes.

'Come on, Ma. Go to your room.'

'No. I'm having fun with you.' Amma sits up straighter.

'Ma.'

She sits up. 'Okay, fine. I'll go. You'll finish my wine?'

'Okay.'

She goes to her room and I walk with her, to make sure she relaxes enough to fall asleep.

*

25

Lavanya takes charge on Day Six.

'Hi, Ami,' she says. Everyone turns around, chairs creaking—I am the last one in, and everyone is only five minutes late. All of them have books open in front of them. Sam has a folded piece of paper in front of her too, filled with her scribbles. It flaps in the breeze.

'Look,' Deeksha says, waving around a biography of Amrita Pritam. 'We're all reading again now.'

'I'm going to talk about Salinger,' Lavanya says. She waves around *For Esmé—with Love and Squalor*, wrapped in library-plastic, coming apart in little triangles at the edges. 'So, I really, really love this book for some reason. And there's one story . . .' She opens it (the plastic cracks) and looks at the contents. '"Down at the Dinghy". That's what it's called. So, basically, there's this kid and his mom is inside this big fancy lake house talking to the housekeeper or whatever, and the kid is in this boat outside the house, sitting there alone. He's sitting in the boat and he just wants to run away. I think it's about the World War, his father is in the war I think, it's set around that time. But then his mother comes out, she keeps trying to pull him out of the boat. And then you realize he really wants to leave, but he just can't. And he can't run away, because it's a lake. It doesn't go anywhere.'

I blink as I repeat everything in my head.

Oh.

It's about me. I can't escape.

Deeksha and Sam watch Lavanya like she is on a TV screen.

'It just makes me so sad because I think that's how we end up thinking sometimes. Sometimes we just feel that way,' Lavanya goes on. 'You end up thinking the same way, you can't stop it even if you want to.'

My insides hum. Is this like looking into a mirror? My hands feel light, unconnected to my body, as I drum on the table. I look at myself like I am not myself but someone else, floating above myself, watching.

'God. I've never thought about it like that before.' Deeksha sits up, impressed. 'I guess it's a good metaphor for mental health. Right?' She then looks at all of us. I'm shaken out of my thoughts.

'Now I want to read this,' Sam says, leaning forward and sliding the book towards herself.

'Lavanya, so well put, I love it,' I say, my voice a little hoarse. She doesn't notice, luckily.

'Oh, no, no . . .' Lavanya lowers her gaze at the creaky wheels on our chairs. 'I still can't write. But at least I can read sometimes.' She gives us a small smile.

'And read so brilliantly, that too,' I say.

I gesture to Deeksha to speak next. 'You want to go next?' I nudge her chair with my foot.

'Okay, yeah. I started reading this book this week. Amrita Pritam, you know, famous writer during the 1930s and everything, and part of the Progressive Writers' Movement, sort of like our own golden age for literature, blah blah, and I read a few chapters. I started thinking, she was so open, so out there, with her personality. She just took these huge steps; she was so confident.' Deeksha looks down at the book, flipping its pages. 'I want to be like that, I think I am like that sometimes, but I don't know if I'm too annoying, when I push people, and try and behave in this confident way . . .'

'Deeksha, come on, I would tell you if you're annoying, you're one of my best friends,' Sam reasons.

'Sam! I literally forced everyone to join my Lit Soc and it lasted like one day before Ami's classes,' Deeksha reasons right back. She frowns. 'And Ami, we had an inter-house dance competition some time back, in August, okay, and I was in charge of the Sarojini House dance. I pushed and pushed and no one even wanted to do my song, and I insisted during every practice, remember, Sam? I keep telling myself it's what makes me me, but what if it's just making everyone hate me?'

I can see Sam and Lavanya move in to speak, but I stop them. 'We can just stay with this moment for now, and talk more about it in a while,' I tell them.

I run my hand across the table: soft and static electric. 'Okay, Sam. Your turn.'

'Okay,' Sam says. She takes in a big, dramatic breath. 'Nobody laugh.' She turns to her bag and pulls out another library-plastic book, rich gold letters, red and blue cover. She places it on the table with a flourish. 'Danielle Steel.'

We all smile at each other. Laughter breaks the air like a crack on ice.

'It just always makes me feel better,' Sam intones, projecting her voice up to the ceiling, arms placed carefully over her book. 'I just feel like it's the perfect way to feel all my feelings at once.'

Everyone's still laughing, and I catch a glimpse of the leaves outside the window, captured between two bars of the window grille: a soft blue-green, moving like waves. My mind wanders back to the oars rowing through the lake. Am I picturing the small boy in the story? Or me?

'Ami, why haven't you read your object poem for us yet? Do that, no?' Deeksha brings me back to earth. Deeksha's face, happy; Lavanya's, wistful; Sam's, energetic; come back into focus.

'It's the last class next time, Ami.' Lavanya jumps in, 'You've postponed it enough!'

'She hasn't even shown me,' Sam adds. 'You have to do it. Today.'

'I will, guys, I will. I mean, I have a draft.'

'Then, read it! You can correct it for next time.'

It's time. I go downstairs, open my email and print out my latest draft. And I come back upstairs.

I read it out. Finally.

In the ten years since Thatha died, images come and go at my window—then they run out, one by one, like cats through an open door.

My sister finishes her homework. I play the keyboard and my sister plays with dolls, for which she has created names, lifestyles, problems. Thatha walks into the room so quietly that my electronic piano drowns it out—I bang down on F sharp and D and A at once. Thatha sits down in the chair and says, 'Continue. Don't let me bother you.' We smile. As if he could ever bother us.

We continue playing and then, when there is a short silence, I realize that his head is tilted. He is looking at us intently.

'How much I love you both, you know?' he asks. He has never said this before, but does that mean we didn't realize it before?

When I look up, Lavanya is looking at me through rippling, molten eyes. 'Firstly, Ami, I really like it,' she says. 'It's so emotional.'

'But you know . . .' Deeksha turns to Lavanya, tapping her pen in staccato beats, 'maybe you could say a bit more, Ami. I mean it's like you're narrating this event, but you don't say why you're narrating it, like what is it bringing out. You have all these objects, but you know, you've tried to write it for ages . . . I mean look at Keats. He talks about the urn, but then also his own feelings about why he's seeing the dancing couple or whatever, why it matters to him.'

I feel so proud of this analysis. Not that I can take credit. It doesn't seem so bad now, my essay, or my mini-essay. Why was I so worried?

Deeksha takes the paper from me. 'That one moment at the end is the only time we really see you. Incomplete conversation.'

'Let me channel Danielle Steel,' Sam says, shutting her eyes, taking a breath, sitting up straight. 'You need to talk about how you feel, Ami, not just what I'm doing or Thatha is saying or something, you need to connect it all together, you know, bring it into an emotional resolution.' She looks around for approval and everyone laughs again.

'Okay, done,' I say. I'm half-scared I'll scratch out all the words when I sit with this essay next, at a half-lit hour of morning or a quiet sunless hour in the evening, when everyone else is buzzing around at home . . . But then again, it's not so scary any more. Plus, I have expert critics who would want to hear my essay again. It's strangely comforting. I feel my thoughts wander away, light, airy, so I bring things back to order. 'Okay, thanks, everyone, now that we're done with my feedback . . . Time for "Tintern Abbey".'

An hour later, I am still feeling light, my thoughts like little paper birds reaching window grilles, tops of dusty cars, my fingertips. I walk out of the library, buy murmuras from Michael at the canteen and walk towards the junior compound. Sam has disappeared upstairs, as have the other girls. I see Akshita walking out of the games room. She lifts her hand, drops it back down: half a wave.

'Hi,' I say.

'Where you going?' Akshita asks. She looks tired: shirt untucked from skirt, hair half-tied, sweat slowly drying on her skin.

'Junior compound.'

'Why aren't you going home?' she asks.

'I'm going, I was just hungry. Want some?' I wave my murmuras at her.

'No, no . . .' Akshita stops, still, near the rose bushes. 'Sorry, I didn't come.'

I look into Akshita's eyes—and she looks at me but a little bit into the distance, like trying to see a very distant ball after she has thrown it.

'It's okay, it's not a real class, you can come if you want . . .' I drift off at the end of my sentence.

She shrugs. 'I do want to, I just . . . Honestly, I'm sure everyone told you, there's this break-up and get-back-together thing with my relationship.' She fiddles with some tiny almond-shaped leaves at the top of the rose bush.

'I know,' I admit.

'And I'm not that good at writing, and the last book I read was my Eco textbook.'

'I know,' I tell her, flicking murmura dust off my fingers. 'When I was in school, I just read the poetry and short story books over and over again. That's why I'm teaching with those. I know them by heart.'

Akshita squints against the sunlight, looks at me. 'I know, we used to use your notes,' she said.

'When I was reading those writers, Keats or Robert Kroetsch or whoever, I just understood it, and it just made me feel like . . .' I fold down the murmuras packet, with the manufacturer address and number stamped on in purple, leaky ink. 'It's like I understood why they wrote it. Plus,

I didn't have to make eye contact with anyone when I was looking at the book.'

I smile and Akshita smiles back. 'You should see my life, I know I talk about the break-up, but still, whenever I go anywhere, that's what people are thinking about me,' she says. She looks at the class 4 kids being marched, in a straight line, to the auditorium.

Somewhere outside the school, a cycle bell rings. Someone's reedy voice bellows out to someone else. We both feel like we need to wrap this moment up.

'God, it's hot,' Akshita says. 'When is the bloody rain coming back? It just came and went this month.'

'I know,' I tell her. 'I'll see you next time, maybe.' Although I don't know if I will. I look up at the clear, absolutely brilliant white-grey sky, and Akshita walks back up the stairs.

*

26

In other exciting news, I finally submitted my history essay. The highest mark I can get is a Pass, 50 per cent, because of how late I am in submitting it. So I am hoping for a Pass, with all fingers crossed.

My latest session with Nirmal ends in a record five minutes, instead of fifteen. I am thankfully coasting on a mild wave. Feeling, but not too much. She says we should just 'keep this current course going' and 'wait for some time before meeting me again, dear.' She gives me her psychologist's number. I fold the torn piece of prescription into an accordion and put it in my phone case.

It's humid outside her clinic. White heat, no clouds, hints of rain: dark grey roads, pools of water near the pavement. The street is quiet, and behind the gates are sleeping watchmen, their radios fuzzy and quiet. I linger before going home. I think maybe this is the kind of moment one should mark in life as a big milestone. I go outside to the park to look for some flowers. As I walk, looking down to avoid the heat,

I think about the time Sam and I put zigzagging gnarly twigs and copper pod leaves in a little hole in the wet mud, as some kind of lucky charm for Thatha to get better again.

In the park, I find some white flowers that grow in thick patches. But who knows if they're weeds or daisies or what? Amma would know. I make my way safely back indoors.

* * *

This week of surprisingly high energy propels me to my final stop. Day Seven of writing class.

I reach before everybody else. I stand for a few seconds in the fresh air, and see the games teacher walking in the distance, wearing his navy trackpants. I wave automatically, and he waves back just as automatically.

I take a deep breath and walk into the library. Deeksha, Sam and Lavanya are sitting in their usual spots, the light falling in golden bars on their faces. I place my tattered FirstBank notebook in the centre of the table: the showpiece.

'How come all of you are on time?' I ask them.

'It's D-Day. The Big Day. The last class,' Sam says.

'We're getting feelings and all.' Lavanya laughs.

I laugh too, and she wheels on her chair.

'So,' I say. 'We did it.'

Deeksha smiles at me, her eyes glimmering, her shoulders leaned back in repose. 'We did it, Ami. Thanks so much for doing this for us.'

'I feel like it was more than just a class,' Lavanya says. 'It was a part of our routine. And we could share a piece of our hearts. So thank you.'

I'm happy she can share how she's feeling with me. My smile hurts my cheeks.

They sway in their chairs and I try to think of what to say, something that's emotional but not embarrassingly so. Sam saves me.

'Okay, read your new draft, Ami,' Sam says.

'Yeah,' Lavanya says. 'I hope you didn't forget? We've been waiting.'

'Please tell me you finally finished it,' Deeksha says.

'Yes, yes. Okay, here goes.'

I open the notebook.

My grandfather died when I was thirteen and nearly seven years later, I am still in that room, hand-washed with lemon disinfectant, fan whirring on the ceiling. I'm still trying to make sense of what happened. Memories almost form, then they leave, like dreams when you lose your sleep in the morning. Or cats running out through an open door, one by one.

Thatha had always been there, in the house, and now he wasn't. I held on to fragments. Something my mother said, something my sister said, the smell of his coconut oil on my dresser. When he was sad and ill, like I am sad and ill, maybe we saw the world the same way. But that's just a romantic idea, one I can never test out because I'd be talking to myself.

I'm not going to arrive at some great solution that will make everything worthwhile. No one magical, full memory-train, Tuesdays-with-Morrie style, that I will turn to, and that will make everything complete.

I want to reach back in time and say something, anything. His evening walk, the way he looks up as I watch TV. Hearing him and Sam talk, being in the other room. His laugh, his slow voice on the answering machine. Thatha died when I was a teenager and I never really got to know him. I got better later, but he was not alive to see those parts. I was too scared to see him in his room. The last day I talked to him, and he remembered who I was, and we had a real conversation, I went out thinking that when I returned to the room, we would be able to continue that. We never did. The Casio keyboard lies up in my cupboard, every key and button turning grey with dust: a silent waltz. And that is the real truth. Things don't add up perfectly; they are left incomplete. The truth is not beautiful; it is just true.

When I open my eyes, Lavanya is the first person to speak.

'Much better.' She nods approvingly.

'Sad, but then everything you write is sad,' Sam says. 'This is sad but *good-sad*.'

'You did it.' Deeksha smiles as she gives me a drum roll, drumming on the table. She turns to Sam confidentially. 'This is what we should use in *KGM Digest*. Shorter.'

'This is perfect,' Sam agrees.

'You know, I really like this one,' I tell them. And I do. This is the version of the essay that feels the most perfect and the least uncomfortable when I read it back to myself. I don't know how I wrote it. I think it's thanks to these girls. The way they believe everything should be from the heart and emotionally satisfying, and how they didn't turn away when I read, but waited, like I should say something more.

'Okay, so now, the moment you've been waiting for,' I say, trying to hide my smile.

'The last poem of these lovely writing classes, before the holidays, is "Tintern Abbey". Perfect last poem. The poem creates a sense of place, and Wordsworth talks about this place he used to go to with his sister. Now that he's returned to it, it's like he remembers something about the way it used to be, how he felt when he was there. I thought we could end on that note.'

Deeksha leans over and traces her finger over the page. 'He's talking about some cliffs and rivers and all.'

'Typical,' Lavanya says. 'Look how pretty flowers are.'

My thoughts connect and collide against each other like bare wire. 'But see, everyone's just talking about the same thing, no matter which era they lived in . . . Hang on, one second, I need to show you something,' I say.

I quietly run downstairs, print out *Wild Geese* by Mary Oliver.

'See.' I place the A4 paper on the table. 'Mary Oliver is also influenced by the natural world and considers herself a Romantic. And look how lovely her poem is.'

'I think I've read this,' Deeksha says.

'See, so this type of writing can be modern too, just a way to connect and share what you think about the world. You see what's outside, which tells you what's inside. It's all the same. Oh, fun fact.' I don't even know how I remember this, but I'm glad it floated up into my consciousness now. 'This was actually Keats' favourite Wordsworth poem. Felt it actually expressed some emotion,' I say. 'The memory by itself isn't interesting. But like you guys just said, Wordsworth conveyed this incredibly sad feeling. He wasn't afraid to share how he really felt.'

Deeksha looks down at her notebook. 'Okay. So "Tintern Abbey" is about some lost world that will never come back?'

'Exactly.'

'So the same old church walls he's seen a thousand times now mean something new,' Lavanya says, holding her grip on the table and swivelling back.

Everyone flips through the poem. Deeksha suddenly pauses.

'Should we call . . .' Deeksha leaves an Akshita-sized blank space in her sentence.

'Not this again.' Sam rolls her eyes without looking up.

'Seriously,' Lavanya says. 'But—'

'But what?'

'I don't know. It's the last class.'

'Listen, I'm not going to beg someone,' Sam says, her face tilting up, looking straight ahead. 'She can come if she wants. She knows where the library is.'

'I'll go,' Deeksha says.

'No, I'll go, I don't mind,' I say and walk out before they can react. I walk into the world, and the auditorium. I see Akshita is in the corner of the choir group, half-singing.

Peace on earth, and mercy mild. The same choir practice Sam is missing to be at my class.

I wave at Akshita. She walks off the stage and comes to see me. We stand near the back of the room and listen to the choir sing. The guitarist joins in at the chorus: *Joyful, all ye nations, rise.*

'Hey.'

'Hey,' Akshita says. She looks brighter now, unlike the day outside Sharon's room. Her face is smooth; her energy seems to be back. That nervous, italics, edge-of-cliff energy.

'Last class, want to come?'

'I'm not sure,' Akshita says, folding her arms and looking out of the auditorium at the freshly chalked field.

'Look, I know things are—'

'A little awkward. Actually, very awkward.'

Say something to relate to this emotional experience.

'So I don't know if I told you this,' I say. 'But you know that room up there?' I point through the window at the abandoned old principal's quarters above the music room, with open, flapping shutters and crows swooping in on branches near it.

'Yeah,' Akshita squints up at it.

'I wasn't in a relationship or anything, but my best friend left school and ditched me, for 11th and 12th and everything. So I used to eat there during break.'

'Alone?' Akshita asks.

'Alone.'

'Oh man.' Akshita plays with the button on her shirt; the blue shirt has turned deep grey around the button, from all the fiddling with it.

'I guess my point is . . . If I had just come downstairs, who knows what would have happened? I mean, people obviously would look at me and talk about me, but they would do that wherever I was, even if I was in the Arctic. Why hide?' I ask her. 'Or maybe this doesn't make sense. I don't know.'

Glory to . . . the newborn king. Each person in the choir ends at a different time; their voices clutter and clash against each other and everyone laughs. They move on to the next song.

You'd better not shout. You'd better not cry. The guitar is a thick river of sound through each word.

Akshita turns to look at the brass latch on the door to the principal's quarters. 'Isn't that locked?'

'Oh, no, it's not actually bolted half the time. I figured that out when I was like eight.'

Akshita looks at me but doesn't really make eye contact. She looks at a stray strand of my hair.

'All right,' I say. 'I'm going to go. Poems to do. All that.'

I wait the appropriate number of seconds before making my exit. Akshita tilts slightly towards the stage, and I think she wants to go back to the ten or fifteen people, one guitarist, dotted across it.

When I am about to turn, Akshita moves slightly—her shirt makes a papery rustle against her arm. 'What poem is it?'

'Oh. So basically "Tintern Abbey" and trying to come up with places that we have some emotional connection to, which we went to in the past, and how it'll be different going back now . . .'

Akshita's shirt is untucked, the sleeves folded; a light layer of sweat lines her hairline like a crown. She smiles.

I'm telling you why . . .

She considers me, eyes moving back and forth. 'Did they ask about me?'

'Yes.'

'What if being there sucks?'

'Then leave. It's just five minutes away from here.'

She smiles, slowly, a spreading watercolour.

'Come,' she says.

So I go.

* * *

Akshita enters the library and stands at the table like she has never been gone. Deeksha and Lavanya look at each other. High alert.

Meanwhile, the sun and the clear pebbles of the rain are moving across the landscapes . . .

'Hi?' Lavanya smiles, a half-smile.

'What's up, guys?' Akshita says, her voice slightly cracking.

Sam doesn't speak, but she doesn't look away either.

'Oh, nothing. We are just . . . we're talking about the *KGM Digest*,' Deeksha says, speaking fast, all her words enjambed.

'So I told her what we're all writing about. Akshita, you can sit down.' I say. Akshita sits at the end of the table.

Deeksha tears out a piece of paper from her notebook, gives it to Akshita, all under ten seconds. Everyone gets back to writing and I estimate the next interruption will be in less than ten seconds. It comes:

'Sam . . .' It's Akshita. 'Umm . . . listen, I'm sorry. I shouldn't have ignored you. It was damn stupid.'

Sam shuffles her feet, swivels her chair. 'I'm sorry too,' she says. 'How are you feeling?'

'Much better. I hope it doesn't change though and . . . I don't know. I hope it stays.'

'At least you're feeling good now.' Sam nods at her.

Ten more minutes to the end of the last class.

'Okay, so . . . only a few minutes to go.' I clear my throat. 'Listen, everyone, I just wanted to say thank you.' I shift in my seat. 'You actually stayed patient and came to all these classes, and I loved all our conversations.'

'Please don't thank us, Ami,' Deeksha says, as if she's just continuing from her last sentence, unstopped. 'You're such a good writer, we should be thanking you.' She talks fast and staccato, arms spread on her chair like a Picasso cat. 'Have you ever thought about getting into teaching?'

I think of what Appa would say. *What, BEd, some 10,000 rupees they'll pay.*

'You think I should?' I ask Deeksha.

'Definitely, Ami.' Lavanya nods at me. She closes her notebook and the topic swerves from me to toasting to the last class. 'We have to do something,' Lavanya says.

Suddenly, a chorus of thank yous, come agains, so goods, so much funs follows.

'Should we go to the beach?' Lavanya asks.

'We could go to my house,' Deeksha says.

'Let's just go to the beach, no,' Lavanya says.

I wish I could go, and I almost picture myself, lighter, marking the moment, like everyone in college, going for a drink after the last class. It feels right, final, but I can't do it. I just can't. I'll lose my steam before we reach the main gate.

I look around. The sandy parking lot stretches out before me. A few people are spread out like ants, carrying bags or eating murmuras or leaning back to catch the sun, like sunbathers.

I turn back to the girls. Time to come clean. However feebly. 'Guys, sorry, I don't think I can come, I feel a little . . .'

'No. Ami, come on!' Lavanya says, her backpack dangling off her shoulder. 'You have to come!'

'I'm sorry, Lavanya, I really wanted to . . . But I'll still be around, so I promise whenever I can, I will. Have fun.' I try and inject my voice with zest.

'You can come for a little while, Ami,' Sam says, her voice lower than the others. She makes sure she is standing next to me, so nobody else hears us.

'I just want to stay here for a while, Sammy.'

'Okay. I'll see you in the evening,' Sam says, and then moves away from me towards the others. 'Come, guys, let's go. We'll just do this again and Ami will come next time.'

They shuffle a little, everyone lingering outside the library, conversations dipping, fading into each other. Finally, they go without me, and I watch until their shadows aren't separate from the shadows of everything else in the distance.

I feel a few stray heartbeats roam around in my chest, marbles skittering on a floor, and I have that brief commentary in my head: *Did I say the right thing, did I not.*

Stop thinking about whether you did or not.

I slowly calm down when I realize that the four of them are too far off for me to join them anyway. The world turns quiet and grey.

* * *

I stand in line at the canteen.

'What,' Michael says when I reach the counter.

'What, "what",' I say. 'Can I have two pizzas?'

'Aiyyo.'

'Last class, okay.'

Michael starts wrapping the pizzas up in thin tissue.

'Actually, three pizzas,' I say. 'You take one.'

'I like brownie.'

'Okay, so take brownie.'

Michael salutes at me. 'Bless you.'

He keeps one nutty brownie, soft, wrapped in tissue, and hands me two delicious pizzas, tiny little circles dripping with spicy, onion-filled red sauce that stains the fingers, capsicum pieces glinting like ocean jewels.

I sit on the rough concrete 'seniors' bench near the canteen and eat.

'Look,' I tell Michael, pointing to the gate. A father is riding by on a scooter with his little daughter, both dressed in nylon-red Santa shirts. The daughter is standing at the front of the scooter, looking out at the road, like she is the one driving. A plastic cover filled with a change of clothes— yellow checked shirt, white vest, a pink T-shirt—hangs off the side of the handlebar. They drive by at a perfect speed, fading like the music in the air.

'Nice,' Michael says. 'That school also had Christmas day, near the main road. Must be from there.'

Right behind the scooter trails a forlorn Santa hat—it flies up and then settles on an almond tree. I wonder if the daughter will miss it—but she has so many in her plastic cover. Michael and I look at the nylon, orange-red hat, fluttering, on the almond leaves, and we make the same decision simultaneously. We run to the gate with our phones, frame the almond tree against the sky, and click the hat hanging against the green.

We walk back and reunite with our food. Michael eats at the canteen counter; I sit on the bench. I stare at the picture on my phone: the rich blue, the green, the little hat, criss-crossed with telephone cable wires.

'So, year finish,' Michael says.

'What's your holiday plan?' I ask him.

'Going back home,' Michael says. 'To Madurai.'

'Oh, that's so nice.'

'My mother will be happy. Anisa also.'

'Who's that?'

'My daughter.' Michael pulls out his billfold and walks towards the bench. 'Look.' He shows me a small picture, a girl with a round face, two ponytails, big excited eyes and a goofy smile, against a green studio screen with bright technicolour flowers.

'Couldn't pick a simple backdrop?' I ask Michael, teasing. I point at the flowers.

'Excuse me, she likes like this only,' he says. 'Best studio in Madurai.' He puts his wallet back into his pocket.

'She's so cute.'

'What cute,' Michael says. 'Every day she will call me in the morning when I'll be coming to KGM. She'll cry, "I can't go to school."'

'Why not?'

'Simply. She doesn't like to go, that's all. So I'll tell her, every day, nothing will happen today, just go and come.' Michael has his hands folded in his lap. 'Then we will go for Mass on Christmas. That she will like. They'll give free cake in church and free toffee.'

'I love her,' I say.

'*Ey, po*,' Michael says and stands up straight. He has to hold his back, steel himself. He exhales. 'I told you, no,' Michael says. 'You will manage full class.'

'Next time I'll do a bigger class and the auditorium will be full.' I salute. 'You wait and see.'

'Come, come,' Michael says. 'We will roam around KGM together.'

Michael starts rearranging things, shuffling and shifting things, behind the counter. I lean back on the bench, with my pizza. Rain falls: light, slow murmurs at the awnings, drips down leaves.

I am not normal, I think, talking to an audience that does not exist, watching Michael wipe down the counter with a wet, checked cloth. *But it's fine. I'm fine.*

Like a portal in front of me, under the neem tree, in the empty expanse of field, I see an early morning, all those years ago. Thatha sitting up on the bed, with his spectacles on, looking up. He slowly pushed himself up by his palms and sat up a little bit straighter against the upright pillows.

'Are you feeling okay?' I asked him.

'Yes, yes, I am feeling fine,' he said. He moved his hand slowly upwards in the air in front of him like he was tracing the incline of a graph. 'You see, for every person, life will go up, up, up.' He changed directions and moved his hand down the fall of an invisible graph. 'And then it will come down.' He slid his hand down the invisible slope until it was flat.

The mesh on the window behind him was attached to the grille by Velcro on all sides of the windowpane. The Velcro was coming slightly apart at the seams. The dust made the golden mesh look almost brown, a faded rust. The neem tree outside the window was bending and moving. The light fell on Thatha's right side, where the hollows on his face seemed deeper.

Thatha closed his eyes again and then opened them.

'Amma is cutting some apple,' I said. 'Do you want?'

'Is it available?' Thatha asked.

'Yeah! There's enough for you!'

'Then please, I will take a little bit,' Thatha said. He tilted his head, and the light glinted against his spectacles, turning one ray in the room golden.

The sky is grey. Dogs are asleep on the median between the gate and the road, outside the school. I try not to let my heart burst into two and spill on to my pizza crust. I hold myself. The feeling of happiness creeps up on me, a slow tide, a wash of salt. Then I try not to name or draw attention to that feeling because if I do, if I get too close, it will go away: a skittish, nervous stray cat.

*

27

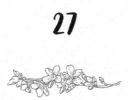

Freshly unemployed, enjoying my minuscule stipend, I am lying on my bed in mid-December. I'm now reading *Letters to a Young Poet* by Rilke. *Ask the questions, don't wait for the answers.* More accurately, the book is upside down on my stomach while I gently nap, eyes half closing, conversation outside a low drone that grows loud. Appa materializes at my door in the early evening.

'Hm,' he says, this time in a plain blue T-shirt and a lungi.

'What?'

'Move.'

I move and Appa lies next to me. I feel small and tiny beside him.

'How are you?' he asks me.

'Fine, why?'

'Anxious?'

'Not right now.'

'So can I ask you a question? You won't get irritated?'

'I never get "irritated", Appa.'

'Did you decide? Reply to Maggie?'

'I didn't reply. Maybe I'll reply. I don't know.'

'Let's go winter shopping,' Appa says.

'Like, now?'

'I have to buy you things, no? You have an empty suitcase. And you never do anything yourself. No planning. Come on, get ready.'

Soon, we are in the car. Outside the window are slowly passing bakeries with browning bread, paan shops and traffic signals. The cotton trees give way to hoardings advertising electronics, sapphire earrings or rental properties on the East Coast Road. Traffic junctions languish in the shade of sweeping flyovers above us. Inside Zara, amidst the winter clothes that would be out of place in Chennai, we prowl around the coats section. Appa asks me to try on a navy blue, heavy coat. It falls to my knees. Its buttons are garish and brassy.

'Try it on properly.'

I pull at the lapel, trying to get the shoulders snugger.

'It's too thick, Appa.'

'This is how people wear them,' Appa says. 'It'll be cold in January.'

'No, Pa,' I say. 'Mostly people wear layers, full-sleeved shirts . . .'

He holds out a camel-coloured puffer coat to me.

'I can't wear this, Pa.'

'You know I only had three outfits stitched for college? Three shirt-pant sets. Thatha got it stitched for me.' He then begins stretching, right there in the middle of Zara, putting his arms on his waist and turning left and right, his body cricking in stiffness.

'I can manage with three outfits,' I say. 'Look.' I pick up a plain black full-sleeved T-shirt, with lint from other people's bags stuck on it like impressionist art. 'Suppose you wear this. Then you wear a sweater. Then a coat. That's enough.'

'Or thermals,' Appa says, leaning against the wall, ignoring the salesperson who is standing there, adjusting his shirt collar in the mirror.

'You gave me ten thermals and I only used them once,' I say.

'Okay at least try this on,' Appa says. He passes me a black coat. It's beautifully square shouldered, large pockets, a warm black. 'This is a smart one. Ey, Thomas.'

Where do they even store these in Chennai? How do they not come apart just from the warehouse to the store? It is a temperate twenty-six degrees outside. My sweat is forming tantric chakra shapes on my back. I try the coat on, and my arms are trapped to my side. The salesperson is jolted awake and he folds his arms. He has a walkie-talkie strapped to his black belt. I wonder what messages are exchanged on those.

'Give me this coat in a bigger size,' Appa says.

'Sir, whatever is on these racks, is our stock,' he says. But then in a moment, he pushes his curly hair out of his eyes and searches on the rack and gives us a size larger.

'Appa, stop calling people Thomas,' I say.

'What else am I supposed to call them? Here,' Appa says and gives me the coat. This time, it fits perfectly, and falls to my waist as if I have some shape.

'It's Rs 8000,' I say, trying to use price as an excuse. 'Who would buy that?'

'Take it, it's nice,' Appa says and walks ahead. I move out of the way of a woman with a large yellow handbag, who frowns at me when my elbow accidentally touches her handbag strap. She is rummaging through the Rs 700 Discount section.

'Here, try this.' Appa holds up a navy blue, striped sweater, which looked like it fits a doll with spindly arms, not a human being.

'Pa. This is not going to fit.'

'Try it on and see.'

'The line for the trial room is long.'

'Try it here then.'

This is Appa. He thinks I can try on a sweater, in public, and risk taking it off and exposing my bare stomach, as a nineteen-year-old, under bright white lighting and in front of two mirrors and tens of people.

'What,' Appa says, rather than asks.

'Nothing, nothing.'

Appa is lingering outside the store, people watching and retying his shoes, while I bill the shirt, sweater (two sizes up from the spindly one) and coat. Upon seeing me, he looks down at his watch. 'We still have to buy winter shoes and one more sweater,' he says. 'Maybe a good pair of jeans. Not your horrible fully torn ones.' He sounds pained. He presses both palms on his neck and stretches, facing the ceiling, with its artificial suns hung up on string, near the furniture and suitcase stores on the third floor.

The air smells of refried patties from the Tibb's stall, microwaved food from Coffee Bean and popcorn from the movie theatre.

'Let's do it next time, no, Pa?'

'Sure?' He is relieved.

'We have some time before dinner,' Appa says in the car. He starts the engine with a series of clicks. 'Want to go for a drive?'

'Aren't you tired? You were stretching in Zara.'

'Feeling better since we left the mall. I hate those places.'

We drive and drive, past the main road and straight towards the city limits near the airport. Here, there is just the slow quietening; the widening of the roads; the sprawling of highways like tendrils; and the metro stations under construction, looming overhead. Appa parks the car on an empty road, just before the airport parking and the sweeping highway leading to Departures. It's wide, still; yellow grass presses up against the edges of the road. We are in Meenambakkam, says the bright navy lettering hanging on a train station painted white, an abandoned grey staircase leading up to it.

'Get down—on this side, not the side near the road,' Appa says.

We stand on the grass and lean against the car. It's stopped raining, and the drizzle turns the sky clear, and clouds blot and block out the sun. Our car blocks some of the sound of the traffic. We are staring at a high, pale yellow wall. It stretches up over ten feet, and there is barbed wire in curlicues all around its top, looping and looping.

'Amma and I used to come here all the time to see planes,' Appa says, looking up at the wall.

I look straight at the wall. I can see the top of a grey aeroplane, just barely before it takes off, but little else. There is just the paleness of the wall, and the barbed wire.

'How? You can't see anything,' I say.

Appa squints against the light and seems confused by the presence of the wall. 'This wasn't there before,' he says. 'It used to be open. There was a small fence and we could directly see the runways. We would park the car here and just sit. Time used to pass like that.'

He takes a breath. 'It was lower,' he says. 'The wall.' Appa stretches his arms and puts one arm on the front bonnet of the car, a golden Honda City.

Without the wall, without the wire, it would have been a quiet spot: the traffic only properly starts further down the road. There would have been open grey space. The noses and the windows and the wings of the planes would all have been clear, as they ascended, as their flight ended. The sky would have been criss-crossed with them.

'When the current at home was gone, we used to put on the AC in the car and drive,' he says.

'It must have been years ago,' I say.

'Yeah. It wasn't like this. Sometimes I just forget, and I think everything is . . .' Appa lifts his weight off the car.

'Should we eat something?' I ask Appa.

'But there's food at home,' Appa says. He looks at his watch. It's almost seven in the evening. 'Where should we go?'

'I don't know. Should we get into the car?'

He frowns at me. 'Can you see any planes?'

I wait, in silence, like a birdwatcher. In a way, circling planes do seem to have a life of their own, and when we see them in the sky, we don't think about how they are operated by people; owned by companies, engineered, loaded with cargo and bad food. They are just soaring things, with blinking lights. The kind of thing people stop and park to look at, and they seem like the most beautiful, rarest, most exciting thing in the world.

The sky is tinged a pale purple and above the barbed wire, I see, finally, a plane move upwards as if it is a feather in the wind. It's a grey line, hazy. The pollution makes the air look like waves of water. The plane bobs, soars and disappears.

'Hey,' I say to Appa, but he isn't looking up. He's looking at a scooter parked near the stairs of the metro station.

'A plane,' I say to myself.

Appa and I stopped to eat idlis and drink coffee at the usual spot: Sangeetha in R.A. Puram. Things I learnt from an internet search in the car: there is a plane watchers club in Chennai. I think about joining it. Maybe I'll be able to tell which plane is which, and start calling them birds. I share this information with Appa while he pours all the three chutneys on to his idli and then eats it. I eat my mini idlis swimming in warm and sweet sambar.

'Sorry,' Appa says. 'I wanted to . . . I just thought. I never know what to do with you. Sam is easy, but you . . . nobody knows. You'll feel something, nobody will know and nobody can ask you anything, you'll just go off into your room. Everything you take the wrong way.' His spoon floats in mid-air. 'Don't mind.'

'I don't mind,' I say. 'But it's not as if I can do anything about it.'

'I know you are finding this difficult,' Appa says. 'But so am I. I don't know what to do.'

'I don't think anyone really "knows", you know,' I say.

'Amma says you're going to a therapist?'

'Yeah. When I find one. Like, an actually good one. Nirmal recommended someone, let's see . . .'

Appa flicks off some dried idli from his fingers. I don't know how to placate him: he seems a bit at sea. So I ask for the bill, and we sit there amidst empty plates, lines of chutney still, like lakes.

'It's okay,' I say. 'I did see a plane. Promise.'

Appa looks up and smiles. He reaches out like he is going to hold my hand, then lifts his hand up instead. 'Two coffees,' he tells the waiter.

Appa takes his wallet out and starts counting his rupee notes, fanning them out like a poker hand.

'Should you be doing this in public?' I ask him.

'If anyone wants to steal, they are welcome to steal my two hundred rupees,' Appa says. 'Told Amma we're coming home for dinner?'

'I'll message her.'

I tap at my phone. Appa laces his hands and regards the passing traffic. The coffee arrives and we sip it, while it's still hot and strong. The black marble on the table reflects my hands back at me. I take another sip and finish the whole cup. The slow traffic steams by endlessly. The tamarind trees spread their branches, like arms, into the sky.

'Do you ever wonder when this sign became universal?' I ask Appa. I hold my finger and thumb five inches apart, in sort of a C-shape, and sip. 'People always do this when they ask for coffee.' I tilt my head to the left. 'See those two people. Just now, they asked.' I make the sign. 'And they said "coffee".'

'Correct,' Appa says. 'Come. Let's pay and go.'

*

Acknowledgements

Poonam Ganglani, who worked with me on early drafts of the manuscript, and taught me about novel structure.

Smit Zaveri, my first editor at Penguin, for believing in, editing and sculpting the book.

My subsequent editor, Arpita Nath, who saw the book through to its completion, and made me see the story clearly.

Copy editor Shalini Agrawal, who sharpened the book and made it so much richer.

Samar Bansal, for designing the cover; the illustrator Nandita Ratan; the marketing team; and everyone else at Penguin for bringing the book—and my dream—to life.

My family, for their patience and good humour. My father, for his imagination. My mother, for her book recommendations. My sister, Shloka, for always being the first and wisest reader.

My friends and beta readers for reading, discussing and rehashing the book over the years: Shishir; Jasmitha, Aashika, for everything; Andrew, for more of everything; MJ; Nomes; Bhavya; Shanna, a wonderful beta reader who gave me so much guidance on the emotional truths in the book, and

Acknowledgements

'youth-speak'; and so many young beta readers who told me what was good and—very honestly—what wasn't.

All those whom I cannot name, and who prefer to be anonymous. So many people I spent time with, learnt from, who stuck with me.

You, the reader.

Thank you to all of you.

READ MORE IN PUFFIN

Unfair by Rasil Ahuja

Life's not always fair . . . and neither are we

Auditions are on for the seventh grade annual play. Lina sets her heart and sights on the lead role, but the drama teacher seems to think Lina isn't the right shade for the part. All Lina wants is a #FAIRCHANCE to try out for the role. Will narrow-minded Miss Deepa derail Lina's dream?

Meher finds maths far more interesting, and less dramatic, than Macbeth. When her extroverted BFF Lina suddenly becomes distraught and withdrawn, Meher tries to figure out what she may have done wrong, but things just don't seem to add up. Will their friendship fade or will Meher find a solution to this problem and score #FRIENDSHIPGOALS?

You Are Simply Perfect! by Sadia Saeed

A self-help guide-cum-journal for self-exploration

Jealousy. Bullying. Anger. Anxiety. Body image issues. Selfies and social media addiction . . . Are you grappling with any of these?

Let's be honest, juggling school, extra classes, home, friendships and new relationships can be hard. It's difficult to find balance and really, *really* tough not to get affected by the 'happy' content we see online. But what is genuine happiness vis-à-vis short-term pleasure? Are we even looking for it in the right place?

Written by a renowned psychologist, this beautifully illustrated book is divided into five parts that will help in easing everyday anxieties. Learn to make friends with yourself, your body, mind and feelings, and to deal with difficult emotions and situations.

You Are Simply Perfect! will equip you with life-changing tools to find contentment—in school and outside. Find your own quiet spaces inside this book with journal pages left for you to write and reflect.